I o

For N
Fan Scor.

A Nvns Begering p
consolisati THE
Ennofu Yerm
—

Loik Nevormi t
Nmy Stin nlukd
Megons

xxx

Dagbo C
Enl Sp

WALKING THE LONDON SCENE

WALKING THE LONDON SCENE

FIVE WALKS
in the footsteps of the
BEAT GENERATION

Including links to The Beatles

Sydney R Davies

Sydly ~../~

The Grimsay Press

The Grimsay Press
an imprint of
Zeticula
57 St Vincent Crescent
Glasgow
G3 8NQ

http://www.thegrimsaypress.co.uk
admin@thegrimsaypress.co.uk

First published 2006

ISBN-10 1 84530 030 0 Paperback
ISBN-13   978 184530 030 2

Acknowledgements

Most of the research comes from the books listed in the bibliography and from various websites. I would like to thank especially Barry Miles for his encouragement and for his two detailed and entertaining books, *The Beat Hotel* and *In the Sixties* (which he obviously does remember; if you need a first class introduction to the works of the wider Beat Generation, then Miles' *Beat Collection* is a fine place to start); Ted Morgan for his seminal work, *Literary Outlaw - The Life and Times of William S Burroughs*; Douglas Lyne for his reminiscences of Burroughs; Christopher Gibbs for confirming my hunches about a certain photo and the editors of the various books of letters, without whom these walks would have been much shorter and a lot less fun. Most of the poems quoted are from Corso's *Long Live Man* and Ginsberg's *Planet News* and it's worth taking copies along to read the poems at the sites that inspired them. My first 'Beat' walk, Kerouac's London, originally appeared in *Moody Street Irregulars* several years ago, but it's thanks to Jules, Ashley, Jerry, Mike, Ric and other fellow London flâneurs, whose company and inspiration made me construct these new walks and put pen to paper.

Contents

Introduction

*In January 1964, William S Burroughs made a trip
to Paris and stopping off in London on the way back
to Tangier for a television interview, he had a nasty
surprise. The customs official at Heathrow checked his
name against a list, crossed out the 'three months' on
his visa, and stamped 'permitted to land on condition
does not stay longer than two weeks.' 'Why have you
come to England, Mr Burroughs?' he inquired. Deadpan,
he replied, 'For the food and the climate'.*
From: *Literary Outlaw - The Life and Times of William S. Burroughs*
by Ted Morgan

The Americans who became known as the
literary movement the 'Beat Generation' were
a well travelled crew. Best known for criss-
crossing the US in search of adventures, 'kicks',
God and each other, they also took merchant
ships to far flung corners of the globe. To the
jungles and deserts of Central & South America
and Africa in search of the 'fellaheen' and exotic
drugs, to the Far East in search of enlightenment
and to Europe for culture, literature and the
Zeitgeist. Often just passing through, sometimes
they stayed for months (or even years); all
returned to America in the end. Probably their
most famous residence in Europe was the
'Beat Hotel' at 9 rue Git-le-Coeur in Paris. But
they did also come to London over a period
stretching from participation in World War II
to readings and signings as late as 1998, with

the most frequent visits taking place in the late 50s and 60s. Apart from William S Burroughs that is. He first came to London as a boy with his parents before the war and actually lived in London off and on for a number of years and, inevitably, on these walks he will feature more often than the others.

There were many writers who were considered to be members of the Beat Generation, but some like Gary Snyder or Philip Whalen looked more to the East than the West for their travels. Therefore these walks concentrate on five of the main protagonists, all of whom came to The Smoke in their wanderings:

William S Burroughs (1914-1997)
Lawrence Ferlinghetti (b.1919)
Jack Kerouac (1922-1969)
Allen Ginsberg (1926-1997)
Gregory Corso (1930-2001)

Although Burroughs lived in London in the late 60s/early 70s, he first came here as an adult in 1956 and was a visitor in the 80s. Corso and Ginsberg came over together from Paris in 1958 and both were around in the 60s with Ginsberg returning for the last time in 1995. Ferlinghetti and Kerouac were the earliest arrivals as war brought over the Yanks and although Ferlinghetti has returned a couple of times for readings, Kerouac only passed through once again in 1957 on his way back from Tangier to fame and fortune in the US.

There are five walks in all, with varying degrees of length, but all should be achievable in a morning or an afternoon. Distances and approximate timings are given, but please note that on some walks short tube rides are required to connect up various locations. However, all the walks are within Zones 1 & 2 of the London Underground system and cheap daily cards can be purchased. Although comprehensive directions and sketch maps (NB not to scale) are given, any good street-by-street map of the city is also recommended. The focus is on 'Beat scene' locations but many other points of interest will be passed on these walks.

Each walk starts and ends at a London Underground station and most will have free local maps of the immediate vicinity to help find the way at the start of the walk. They all end with a recommended pub or two where you can rest your weary legs and raise a toast to the writers who inspired a generation.

Walk 1: West London
6 Miles - 3-4 Hours

Starting in pleasant gardens, this walk leads on to a great literary event, a mysterious Doctor and an (in)famous hotel, carries on with tales of drink and addiction before traversing a cemetery and ending on a bridge.

Walk 2: North London
8 Miles - 4-5 Hours

This walk goes down many elegant streets, through two parks via a mosque and an engine shed to reach a graveyard at the end. It is probably the most 'Beatle-ish' walk and we will meet several other animals and notable poets along the way.

Walk 3: Fitzrovia, Bloomsbury and Soho
3.5 Miles - 2-3 Hours

This is a short stroll through a departed literary history. Fitzrovia was 50s London's answer to the older Bloomsbury set and we pass the places where maverick publishers and booksellers used to ply their trade. However, Soho still hangs on to its seedier side, despite several attempts to clean the place up, as the observant walker will discover.

Walk 4: St Paul's to St James's
4.5 Miles - 2-3 Hours

Lots of historical City places to see on this walk, with diversions down an alleyway and a hidden yard and ending with a regal flourish. A key Burroughs site features heavily towards the end.

Walk 5: South West London
6 Miles - 3-4 Hours

From the busy worlds of Brixton and Victoria Station to the quieter atmospheres of a gallery and a tangle of Chelsea streets, this walk starts at a cinema and has blue plaques and personal anecdotes by the bucketful.

West London

START

KEY
1. Francis Bret Harte
2. Peter Pan
3. Physical Energy
4. Albert Memorial
5. Royal Albert Hall
6. Hand & Flower
7. Samuel Taylor Coleridge
8. Hotel Rushmore
9. Earls Court Exhibition Centre
10. Empress State Building
11. Hotel Lily
12. Lillie Langtry
13. Brompton Cemetery
14. Chelsea & Westminster Hospital
15. Goat in Boots
16. Pan Bookshop
17. Royal Marsden

LEINSTER TCE
SLOANE ST
LANCASTER TCE
LANCASTER GATE
BAYSWATER ROAD
LANCASTER GATE

THE SERPENTINE

GALLERY

BUS 9, 10, 52
KENSINGTON GORE

ADDISON RD
HOLLAND RD
KENSINGTON HIGH ST
WARWICK ROAD
ADDISON BRIDGE PL
WARWICK GDNS
PEMBROKE RD
CROMWELL GDNS
CROMWELL ROAD
WARWICK ROAD
TEMPLETON PL
TREBOVIR RD

EARLS COURT

EARLDOM PL
OLD BROMPTON ROAD
WEST BROMPTON
FINBORO RD

SOUTH KENSINGTON
SYDNEY PLACE

DRAYTON GDNS
REDCLIFFE GDNS
FINBORO RD
FULHAM ROAD
EDITH GROVE
CALLOW ST
PARK WALK

BUS 14

BUS 14
RIVER
PUTNEY BRIDGE
THAMES
PUTNEY BRIDGE

END

Walk 1
West London
6 Miles - 3-4 Hours

Exit Lancaster Gate tube station on the Central Line and turn right on Lancaster Terrace.

Further up, No. 52 has been demolished and Maitland Court may now be on the site. This was where English publisher Marion Boyars had a flat and Burroughs sub-let from her. He also lived in a flat at No. 5 (now part of the hotel opposite on the corner of Gloucester Terrace) with Ian Sommerville from March to June 1962, before decamping back to Paris and the Beat Hotel.

Go down to Bayswater Road and turn right, crossing at the lights and then right past *The Swan* pub and right again into Lancaster Gate and follow it as it turns left. Walk down to the end passing *Spire House* (an old church) and a war memorial to the end. Turn right at Leinster Terrace and stop just around the corner on the right at No.   74 Lancaster Gate.

There is a blue plaque here to Francis Bret Harte (1836-1902). J. Kingston Pierce in *San Francisco, You're History!* claims that Bret Harte's witty, sometimes heart-rending tales of frontier California earned him acclaim during the 1860s as the 'new prophet of American letters'. Eastern magazines courted him for submissions and no less a critic than San Francisco's own Ambrose Bierce (author of *The Devil's Dictionary*) called his humour 'incomparable'. The highlights of Harte's oeuvre - from *The Luck of Roaring Camp* to *The Outcasts of Poker Flat* and *Mliss*, helped establish the foundations of western American fiction. Could he be the first Beat on the West Coast?

**About turn and walk down Leinster
Terrace to Bayswater Road, turn left
crossing over at the lights and walk back
to the entrance to Kensington Gardens at
Marlborough Gate.**

On your left beyond The Serpentine (actually
part of the Westbourne river) and adjoining the
Gardens, is Hyde Park where Ginsberg, together
with poets Brian Patten and Adrian Henri, read
at a rally demanding the legalisation of marijuana
on 16th July 1967.

**Go ahead keeping the lake on your left
and just after the Peter Pan statue, turn
right and take the first fork right towards
a junction of paths with an equestrian
statue in the middle (*Physical Energy* by
George Frederick Watts). From here
bear slightly left and go ahead towards
the Albert Memorial, with Prince Albert
seated in his golden splendour and the
Serpentine Gallery on your left. (Look
out for the sculpture of Shakespeare with
a book in his hand). Stop on the steps
on the other side of the Albert Memorial
opposite the Royal Albert Hall.**

This is most famous in Beat terms as the
venue for the great literary event of 1965, the

International Poetry Incarnation, sometimes
known under the film title *Wholly Communion*.
But first, we must note that in 1943, during
World War II, at the tender age of 21, Kerouac
came to England on a merchant ship. After
docking in Liverpool, he ventured down to
London, just like any other American sailor. In
Vanity of Duluoz, he describes his visit to the Hall:
'Then I doodled around looking at posters
and decided to try Royal Albert Hall for that
evening for a performance of Tschaikowsky by
the people there with Barbirolli conducting.
As the concert was going on, and I sat in the
balcony next to an English soldier, he whipped
out a volume of verse by T S Eliot called Four
Quartets and said they were magnificent. Lot I
cared.'
A month or so before the poetry event, Bob
Dylan invites Ginsberg to join him in performing
at the Hall and to a party with the Beatles
thereafter. Noticing a very tense gathering, he
nestled up to Dylan only to have John Lennon
chide, 'Why don't you get closer!' Not missing a
beat, Ginsberg fell into Lennon's lap with '... have
you read William Blake?' This was also the time
Ginsberg appeared in the opening credits of D A
Pennbaker's film of Dylan, *Don't Look Back* (Walk
4).
England! awake! awake! awake!
Jerusalem thy Sister calls!

According to Barry Miles in his book, *In the Sixties*, while sitting around at Better Books (Walk 3) Ginsberg said that Ferlinghetti and Corso would be arriving in London soon and he wanted to organise a reading similar to the 1956 affair he arranged in Berkeley, California. All the venues suggested seemed too small, so Barbara Rubin asked: 'What's the biggest joint in town?' When told it was the Royal Albert Hall, she promptly picked up the phone and booked it for ten days' time. Miles said: 'It needed American *chutzpah* and knowhow to think that big'. In a letter from Paris to James Laughlin, publisher of New Directions, Corso said: 'I am seeing Larry here in Paree and he is truly gentle soul. We go to London to read with Ginsberg and Russian poet, the fine one, Voznesensky, plus Lamantia. So that should be something. I haven't read in years and at Albert Hall of all regal places!'

A press conference was held on the steps of the Albert Memorial announcing the event, which made it onto the news. On 11th June 1965, the biggest poetry reading ever held in the UK drew 7,000 spectators. Radical psychiatrist R D Laing (and some of his patients!), Nobel Laureate Pablo Neruda and the future Prime Minister of India, Indira Gandhi were in the audience. There were performances from nineteen poets, including Ginsberg, Ferlinghetti, Corso, Adrian Mitchell, Michael Horovitz, Alexander Trocchi, Christopher Logue, Jeff Nuttall, Andrei Voznesensky, Harry Fainlight, Simon Vinkenoog and Ernst Jandl.

Peter Whitehead, who filmed the event (released by Lorrimer Films), said in an interview in *The Guardian* in 2002: 'There was a breathtaking optimism in the International Poetry Incarnation at London's Royal Albert Hall - electricity in the air and ecstasy in the hearts. As Allen Ginsberg read, one young girl rose to her feet and began moving slowly in a weird twisting dance, a marvellous moment. This vignette and others that characterised the whole crazy, joyous atmosphere was caught in *Wholly Communion*, a film that in intention and feeling prefigures Monterey Pop and Woodstock.' However, when it was sent it to the BBC, a curt letter was sent back stating: 'Thank you very much for showing me *Wholly Communion*, the film of the International Poetry Reading. In my opinion it is the worst film I have ever seen in my life.' It has still not been shown to this day on British television.

In Miles' flat in Hanson Street (Walk 2), with just three days to go, Ginsberg wrote *Who Be Kind To* (from *Planet News*) especially for the occasion. It is a long poem, but worth reading in full for a flavour of the event and bearing in mind the Beatles connection, one line says: 'the boom born that bounces in the joyful bowels as the Liverpool Minstrels of Cavernsink'. Being Ginsberg, there are many references to bodily parts which reportedly drew the comment from the manager of the Hall: 'I don't want that sort of filth here. Would you send your teenage daughter to hear that sort of thing?' On the strength of this event, Miles and his friend, John 'Hoppy' Hopkins (whose photo of Ginsberg adorns this book) decided to start *International Times* (IT) the alternative newspaper of the 60s.

But before we leave the Hall, there are two other connections. Ginsberg read here again in October 1995 before the reading in Heaven (Walk 4) and Paul McCartney came on stage to accompany him on guitar when he read Ballad of the Skeletons. Finally, rock music's most celebrated musicians gathered here on 29th November 2001 to pay tribute to George Harrison on the first anniversary of his death.

Go down to Kensington Gore, turn right and walk all the way up to Kensington Road to Kensington High Street, passing Queen's Gate, Kensington Church Street, Holland Park and the Commonwealth Institute to stop at the junction with Addison Road and Warwick Gardens (if this doesn't appeal, a number 9, 10 or 52 bus will chop a mile/30 minutes or so off the walk).

Down Addison Road, the house at No. 24, formerly the home of Dr Dent, is no longer there. Dr Dent was known for curing alcoholics, including English writer Patrick Hamilton, the author of *Hangover Square* (though sadly in his case he failed). Second hand copies of his book, *Anxiety and Its Treatment, with Special Reference to Alcoholism* can still be picked up. Ted Morgan in *Literary Outlaw - The Life and Times of William S. Burroughs* says: 'At the start of 1956, Burroughs took stock of his situation. The last two years had been a blur of drugs. His attempts to kick had failed, and once again he had a heavy habit. He had heard about a doctor in London who treated addicts, and prevailed upon his parents to send him $500 to go to Dr Dent at 24 Addison Road. The entire treatment lasted fourteen days, and for the first four days and four nights, Burroughs couldn't sleep. He hated London, which seemed to him overregulated. He had seen a sign in a pub that said: "No liquor may be consumed after time is called. Drinking must stop at once, no time being allowed for consumption". So when time was called, Burroughs supposed, you had to spit your drink out on the bar.'

In a letter to Ginsberg dated 8th May 1956 from Egerton Gardens (Walk 5), he said: 'I still feel terrible. Sleep maybe 1, 2 hours at dawn. I can walk for miles and come in stumbling with fatigue but I can't sleep. Last night went to a ghastly queer party where I was pawed and propositioned by a 50-year-old Liberal MP.' And on 15th May: 'I am completely recovered now, very active, able to drink. Still no interest in sex. I am physically able you dig, just not innarested. Ratty lot of boys they got here anyhoo. London drags me like a sea anchor. I want to see bright blue sky with vultures in it. A vulture in London would be an Addams cartoon. But I won't leave until I dig what's here. Dropped Seymour [Wyse] a line. Hope to see him.' Burroughs said that without the treatment offered by Dr Dent, *Naked Lunch* would never have been written.

Continue on ahead across Holland Road and over the bridge with the District Line below and cross over to turn left into Addison Bridge Place by the Hand & Flower pub.

At No. 7 there is a blue plaque on the home of Samuel Taylor Coleridge (1772-1834), poet and opium addict, maybe even a proto-Beat?

For he on honey-dew hath fed
And drunk the milk of Paradise
        From: Kubla Khan

Return to the Addison Road/Warwick Gardens junction (*NB: Not Warwick Road*) and turn right into Warwick Gardens. Follow the street round as it bends left then turn right into Cromwell Crescent. Cross Cromwell Road at the lights and turn left and then right into Templeton Place. At the end, turn left and stop at No. 11 Trebovir Road.

This is the Hotel Rushmore. Burroughs stayed here when he returned to London in January 1966. There was a murder on his train into town from Gatwick airport, which he saw as an ominous sign.

About face and walk down to Warwick Road, turn left, passing Earls Court tube station and then cross over and go down Eardley Crescent to the end. At Old Brompton Road, turn right passing West Brompton tube station. On your left is The Lillie Langtry pub and the Hotel Lily.

The Hotel Lily is on the site of the old Empress Hotel. Following a drug bust in Paris in April 1960, Burroughs moved here and alternated between London and Paris for the next three years, staying in rooms 7, 8, 28, 29, 35 and 37 at the Empress and rooms 15, 18, 29, 30, 31 and 32 at the Beat Hotel in Paris (as documented by Miles). Asked by Victor Bockris what prompted a move to London in 1966, Burroughs replied 'Nothing in particular. I knew people there. It had been a pleasant place. It deteriorated shortly after that. The more positive times I had in London were in the early 60s when I was in and out.' Antony Balch's film depicting the daily lives of Burroughs and Brion Gysin, *Guerrilla Conditions*, was partly shot in these hotels, in

Tangier and in the Chelsea Hotel in New York. However, the film was never completed, though sections appeared in *The Cut-Ups*.

According to Ted Morgan, during his time here, Burroughs lectured to the Heretics Club in Cambridge on the cut-ups. His lover, technician extraordinaire (and joint inventor with Brion Gysin of *The Dream Machine*), Englishman Ian Sommerville, was in his last year there. It was Sommerville who often initiated electronic effects and the use of multiple tape recorders and street recordings. He also worked on *The Cut-ups*. For instance, *Permutations from The Third Mind* were randomly programmed 'poems' printed by Sommerville on a Honeywell Series 200 computer. He appears as 'The Subliminal Kid' in *Nova Express*. The album *Nothing Here Now But The Recordings: Last Words of Hassan Sabbah* (sic) (Industrial Records, 1981) was mostly recorded here in 1960-61. Hassan-i-

Sabbah, 'The Old Man Of The Mountain' was the leader of a fanatical fraternity in the eleventh century AD that lent its name, the 'hashasheen' to the concept of assassination. The text by Burroughs is an expansion of a section in *Nova Express* and was intended to illustrate a condition of advanced paranoia. Burroughs lived quietly here, writing his next novel, *The Soft Machine*, a cut-up work based on material left over from *Naked Lunch*. For relaxation, he would spend a quiet afternoon in the nearby Brompton Cemetery. Apparently, you couldn't find a more pleasant place to sit in all London.

However, he was not unknown in London; the fame of *Naked Lunch* had gone before him, as it was banned in the UK. In an interview in Salon, the English writer J G Ballard, when asked how he had first encountered Burroughs' work, said: 'I think it was in something like 1960. A friend of mine had come back from Paris where *Naked Lunch* had been published by the Olympia Press, which was a press that specialized in sort of low-grade porn, but also published what were then banned European and American classics. I read this little book with a green cover, and I remember I read about four or five paragraphs and I quite involuntarily leapt from my chair and cheered out loud because I knew a great writer had appeared amidst us.'

My friend, Douglas Lyne, archivist and Chelsea habitué of those days, tells a delicious story about how he first met Burroughs in The Lillie Langtry pub next door (still a good old fashioned Irish boozer).

'I visited Paris with my wife Monica in 1963 and there on the quayside was a bookstall of Olympia Press books. These were usually pornographic titles banned in the UK. I picked up a copy of a book called *Naked Lunch* and took it back to the hotel room. As I was expecting something else, my initial view was that it was unreadable and it irritated me, however Monica thought it was hilarious. On returning to London I discovered that Burroughs was the talk of the town. I still have the article from the London Evening Standard dated 7th March 1963, titled *Where Is This Man Heading? The Elusive Mr Burroughs Grants A Rare Interview*. I mentioned Burroughs to George Lamming (author from Barbados of *In The Castle of My Skin*) and he said he thought he was living in London. I asked if he could get in touch with him as I would like to get my copy of *Naked Lunch* signed and he immediately phoned his editor Arthur Boyars and I was given the phone number of the Empress Hotel. I telephoned the hotel and was informed that Burroughs was out but I could leave a message, which I duly did. The very next morning I received a call from a man with the accent of a Southern Colonel - Burroughs. He said that he understood that I would like to meet him, I said that was correct and he said "How about tonight?" He said to meet at the pub near the Empress Hotel at 7.40. I asked if I could bring my wife and he replied "I'd be sorry if you didn't." Monica then got rather agitated - just what should she wear to meet a junkie! We arrived by taxi at around 7.30 and he arrived at precisely 7.40. Following introductions, I asked if he would like a drink and he replied, "That's what we're here for." He ordered a brandy and I then inquired if he could do a double and he replied, "I could do a triple." I think he must have drank at least five triple brandies during the evening before I ran out of money. I can't remember all the conversation, but it was mostly about books, writing and people we might know. I do recall Monica saying that her father had written a successful book (Arthur Grimble - *A Pattern of Islands*) and Burroughs saying that such books were dangerous. Asked why, he replied that "It makes you colonials look attractive, but you're actually really just a bunch of desperados." He was an absolutely arresting figure, very charming and knew what he was talking about. Before we left I invited him to come and meet us in our local (The Surprise in Chelsea - Walk 5) and we fixed up a date.'

Turn around and go back past West Brompton tube again (from here you can take a short cut to go directly to Putney Bridge on the District Line and the end) and turn right through the magnificent portico into Brompton Cemetery.

There's lots of Victorian worthies and war heroes buried here but no literary giants.

Go straight through by either going ahead down the central avenue and turning left at the end or turn left immediately and then right to reach the exit on Fulham Road. Note the sign on the gate as you leave - 'The public are permitted to walk in the cemetery daily' - turn left and cross Finborough Road.

In the booklet which accompanied *The Final Academy* (Walk 5), there is a curious reference to 282 Fulham Road (now a Dry Cleaners). Apparently in these premises in 1968 two people operated a computer which (supposedly) responded to questions from an entity called Control that transmitted from Venus! It is claimed that Balch introduced Burroughs to them and he used the information gathered in *Ah Pook Is Here*.

Cross Redcliffe Gardens and stop outside No. 266 Fulham Road.

This is the site of the old *Cafe Des Artistes*, started by Pete Brown and Michael Horovitz. The place was a hangout for poets and musicians, and was eventually closed down due to drug notoriety. Corso and Anselm Hollo read here at a Live New Departures event in 1962. Horovitz is still publishing his *New Departures* magazine today.

Continue on past the Chelsea & Westminster Hospital and The Goat in Boots pub, to stop opposite Callow Street, where at Nos. 158-162 is the Pan Bookshop.

The closest I ever got to one of the Beats was here in October 1982 when Burroughs (who was here for *The Final Academy*) signed my UK first editions of *Naked Lunch* (John Calder, 1964), *Cities of the Red Night* (John Calder, 1981) and a new paperback, *A William Burroughs Reader* (Pan Books, 1982). He was his usual dapper self in suit and hat and was willing to sign anything thrust in front of him. On my visit for this walk, they had four Burroughs titles, four Kerouac, one Ginsberg, one Ferlinghetti, but unfortunately no

Corso. I bought a Ferlinghetti title, *San Francisco Poems* which, co-incidentally, has a photo of him with Burroughs doing a signing in his City Lights bookstore. Also photos of him with Corso and Ginsberg at other times and crouching over Kerouac's grave in Lowell, Massachusetts.

Continue up Fulham Road and just past the cinema on the left is Drayton Gardens.

On the other side, next to Donovan Court (not that Donovan surely?) is a nondescript garage, where once stood the Paris Pullman cinema. Balch's film, Towers Open Fire, shot in the early 60s in Paris, Gibraltar and London, was premiered here in 1966 alongside Tod Browning's 1932 feature Freaks. It was also screened, along with *The Cut-Ups*, during the launch party for *International Times* at The Roundhouse later that year (Walk 2).

Return to Fulham Road and continue ahead (or cross over and take the No. 14 bus to Putney Bridge) past the Brompton and Royal Marsden hospitals to turn left into Sydney Place and continue along Onslow Square to reach South Kensington tube station. Take the Wimbledon branch of the District Line to Putney Bridge station.

THE SAVING QUALITY

Bad nights of drunk
Make bad days of sorry
Last night was stained with fear
I or the world was all wrong
Today in hard wind and rain
I stand on Putney's bridge
flinging Ritz crackers at the swans
ducks and gulls below
assuring myself Day or night
             I'm all right
   Gregory Corso - Long Live Man (1962)

Up river are the Olympic Studios in Church Road, Barnes, where in May 1967 The Rolling Stones recorded the legendary song *We Love You*.

Allen Ginsberg was in attendance. He wrote to Peter Orlovsky: 'Last night I spent at recording studio with Mick Jagger, Paul McCartney and John Lennon looking like Botticelli graces singing together for the first time. I conducted through the window with Shiva Beads and Tibetan oracle ring.' Even further out in West London lies Her Majesty's Prison in Wormwood Scrubs. In 1967 Ginsberg visited Hoppy who was incarcerated there for drugs. He didn't have a visitor's pass, but the guards thought he must be Hoppy's rabbi and they let him in. If you really want to see the place, you'll have to take the District Line to Notting Hill Gate, change to the Central Line for East Acton and the prison is a short walk away on Du Cane Road. I don't recommend it.

Up river on the Putney side of the Thames is my local, The Duke's Head, at 8 Lower Richmond Road. If it's a summer's day, you can stand outside with your pint of Young's beer and watch the pleasure boats go by. Summer or winter, I might be found in the plain, but warm and friendly, street side bar.

North London
Part One

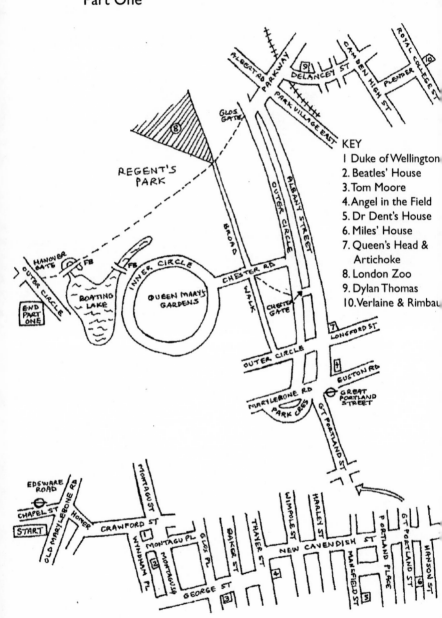

KEY
1 Duke of Wellington
2. Beatles' House
3. Tom Moore
4. Angel in the Field
5. Dr Dent's House
6. Miles' House
7. Queen's Head & Artichoke
8. London Zoo
9. Dylan Thomas
10. Verlaine & Rimbau

Walk 2
North London
8 Miles - 4-5 Hours

Take the District or Circle Line to
Edgware Road and exit onto Chapel
Street. Turn left and cross Old
Marylebone Road at the lights and bear
right into Homer Street, then left into
Crawford Street and walk ahead (look out
for the Duke of Wellington peeking from
the window of the pub of the same name
on the corner of Wyndham Place). At the
junction with Upper Montagu Street with
chemist Meacher, Higgins & Thomas on
the corner (note splendid Victorian lamp
above), turn right, cross Montagu Place
into Montagu Square and, close by on the
left is No. 34.

In 1965 Paul McCartney wanted to start an audio magazine and hired Ian Sommerville to be the editor. They needed an office and as the basement flat at No. 34 (which belonged to Ringo Starr) was empty, they used that. McCartney and Lennon often dropped in, but the magazine never got off the ground and Ian ended up living here for a while (before moving in with Burroughs in Duke Street - Walk 4). Burroughs marvelled at the studio, which had equipment to rival the BBC and he made many hours of recordings here. He once met McCartney by chance, who played the acetate of the *Rubber Soul* album for him. This is also where John and Yoko were living when they were busted for drugs and the nude photo for their album *Unfinished Music Volume One - Two Virgins* was taken here. Jimi Hendrix lived in the flat for a time and wrote *The Wind Cries Mary* here.

Continue ahead, passing a plaque for author Anthony Trollope (1815-1882) at Nos. 38/39, to the other end of Montagu Square, go left on George Street and cross Gloucester Place. On the right, at No. 85 George Street, there is a blue plaque for Irish poet Tom Moore (1779-1852).

Moore had a close friendship with Lord Byron and he wrote about him and his mistresses in his 'journal', a diary he kept for nearly thirty years. Byron left his memoirs to Moore, who sold them to the publisher John Murray. These memoirs discussed Byron's sexual exploits up to the summer of 1816 and were sent to Moore in 1819. They were later ceremoniously burnt at Murray's home in the presence of Moore and John Cam Hobhouse. It has been said that the burning of these memoirs was one of the greatest disasters that English literature has sustained through 'the misplaced scruples of well meaning people'.

Continue ahead to the end, crossing Baker Street, to the junction where Thayer Street meets Marylebone High Street with the Angel in the Field pub directly in front. Turn left, then cross at the zebra crossing to go first right into New Cavendish Street. Go straight across Wimpole Street and Harley Street and then turn right into Mansfield Street where, on the left past Duchess Street, at No. 2 (with the blue plaque to Sir Robert Mayer) we meet Dr Dent again (Walk 1).

In October 1958 Jacques Stern asked Burroughs to accompany him to London to take the Dent cure and Burroughs agreed (since Stern was footing the bill). After taking the cure, Stern rented a flat here but soon enough developed a craving for drugs and sent Burroughs out to make the buys. In a letter to writer Paul Bowles, Burroughs wrote: 'This writing finds me in London, taking the cure with a junkie friend. Since Dr Dent only takes two patients at a time, there are no alcoholics about to lower the tone of the establishment.'

Go back to New Cavendish Street, turn right and cross Portland Place, Great Portland Street and Great Titchfield Street to turn right into Hanson Street.

Barry Miles and his girlfriend Sue lived at No. 15 in a tenement flat on the right called Clevedon House. Ginsberg stayed with them in 1965. He had a natural curiosity. Not knowing much about English life, when the man who came to empty the gas meter, who was standing with his back to him on a chair, turned round to answer Ginsberg, he was standing there with only his socks and shoes on. Ginsberg celebrated his 39th birthday here on 3rd June, where he got completely drunk and ended up with his baggy underpants on his head and a hotel 'Do Not Disturb' sign hung on his penis. At that moment, John Lennon and George Harrison arrived with Cynthia and Patti. Although friendly enough, they seemed embarrassed and only stayed for a short period. Corso also passed through (and passed out once) in 1965, as did Ferlinghetti, when he did his reading at Better Books (Walk 3). McCartney was a regular visitor and Miles lent him copies of Beat material, including *Evergreen Review* and *Call Me Burroughs*.

Return to New Cavendish Street and turn left, at Great Portland Street turn right and continue on to the end, then go ahead, keeping the tube station on your right. Cross the main Marylebone Road/Euston Road junction at the lights and go ahead into Albany Street with the church on your right. On the corner of Albany Street and Longford Street is the Queen's Head & Artichoke at Nos.30-32.

Corso was knocked out by pub names in London when he arrived in 1961. In a letter to Ginsberg he wrote: 'London is lovely the street names the pub names QUEENS HEAD and ARTICHOKE all like that. When I arrived I went direct to Bill's and there in that smoky room was Mike [Portman], Ian [Sommerville] and Bill [Burroughs].'

Continue up Albany Street and cross the road at the pedestrian crossing to go left into Chester Gate by the Chester Arms pub. Cross Outer Circle and enter Regent's Park. Go over the first crossing of paths and bear right to the Broad Walk, turn right and cross Chester Road and go ahead to reach an elaborate drinking fountain (a donation from one Sir Cowasjee Jehangir) and just past this on your left is a corner of the zoo.

DIRECTION SIGN IN LONDON ZOO

⇐
Giant Panda
Lions
Humming Birds
Ladies

Gregory Corso - Selected Poems (1962)

Bear right down an avenue of trees, passing a playground to exit at Gloucester Gate. Cross Outer Circle again and go ahead to Albany Street, turn left, then straight ahead at the crossroads and right over the railway tracks to Delancey Street, stopping at No. 54 on the left where there is a blue plaque for Dylan Thomas (1914-1953).

The famous Welsh poet was introduced by the Scottish poet Ruthven Todd to the White Horse Tavern in New York, a well known Beat hangout. He was soon quaffing oceans of whisky and ale in the back room. Thomas made the place his headquarters on his tumultuous stateside forays and soon tourists were lining up eight deep at the bar to watch him carouse. Today another plaque on the wall of the White Horse commemorates the night in November 1953 when the poet, still only 39, downed one last shot, staggered outside and collapsed. After falling into a coma at the nearby Chelsea Hotel, he ended up in St. Vincent's Hospital where he died. While Kerouac was living in a dilapidated Westside townhouse with the model Joan Haverty, writing On The Road on a roll of teletype paper, he also used to drink so heavily at the White Horse that he was 86'd [barred] a number of times. In his book Desolation Angels he describes discovering 'Go Home Kerouac' scrawled on the bathroom wall.

A 15-20 minute further diversion will take in the house where poets Verlaine and Rimbaud lived. Continue to the end of Delancey Street and turn right on Camden High Street.

Note that from 1968 to 2000, from 234 Camden High Street, the wonderful Compendium Bookshop used to ply its trade. This used to be a great place to buy imported Beat and American literature and lots of writers did signings here, including Burroughs and Ferlinghetti.

Turn first left into Plender Street. Continue on crossing Camden Street to the junction of Royal College Street. Immediately opposite on the house at No. 8 is a plaque stating: The French Poets Paul Verlaine and Arthur Rimbaud Lived Here May-July 1873.

Rimbaud lived in several different places in London during the fateful years of 1872-1874 and it is said that he may have written parts of *Une Saison en Enfer* (*A Season in Hell*) and Illuminations while he was here - 'as rare as pedestrians on a London Sunday morning' (from Cities [II] in Illuminations). The first English translation was published in 1932 by Faber & Faber with an introductory essay by Edith Sitwell (Walk 4). The house still looks pretty much the same as in their day, with peeling paintwork and broken windows. They argued and fought all the time they lived here and we can only imagine how Verlaine must have felt when he noticed Rimbaud standing observing him through the upper window and sniggering as he returned with a bottle of oil in one hand and a fish in the other. Rimbaud got the fish across his face. It was not long after this period in London that Verlaine shot Rimbaud in the wrist in Brussels. Kerouac was a huge fan of Rimbaud and published a broadsheet poem called simply *Rimbaud* in 1960 (it also appears in the *Scattered Poems* volume published by City Lights). Burroughs also told Victor Bockris: 'I'd say Rimbaud is one of my influences, even though I'm a novelist rather than a poet. I have also been very much influenced by Baudelaire, and St.-John Perse, who in his turn was very much influenced by Rimbaud. I've actually cut out pages of Rimbaud and used some of that in my work. Any of the poetic or image sections of my work would show his influence.' As Bob Dylan put it in his song, *You're Gonna Make Me Lonesome When You Go:* 'Situations have ended sad - relationships have all been bad - mine've been like Verlaine's and Rimbaud's.'

Return via Gloucester Gate to the park and the drinking fountain and cross the park in a south west direction, keeping the boating lake on your left and with the tower of the London Central Mosque as your guide. Cross the two blue footbridges by the boat house and exit at Hanover Gate.

North London
Part Two

KEY
1. London Central Mosque
2. Panna Grady's House
3. Lord's Cricket Ground
4. Paul McCartney's House
5. Abbey Road Studios
6. The Roundhouse
7. Wesley's Chapel
8. Bunhill Fields

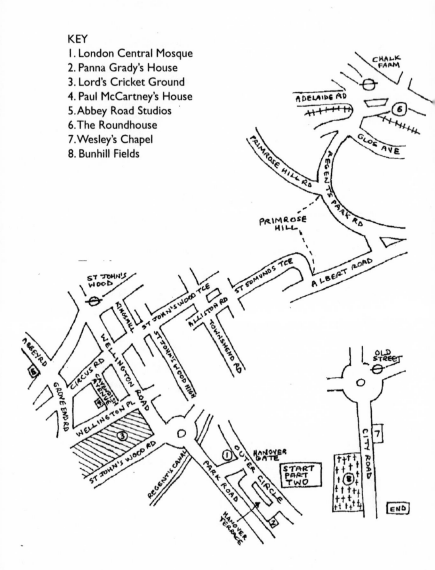

**Cross Outer Circle for the last time and
slightly to the left is Hanover Terrace.
Go down to the end of the terrace
passing blue plaques to author H G Wells,
architect Anthony Salvin and composer
Ralph Vaughan Williams. At the end under
one of the grand porticos and columns is
No. 2.**

In 1967, Ginsberg lodged with Panna Grady
and the great American poet, Charles Olson
here. Panna was a socialite and once ran a
literary salon in the Dakota building in New York
(outside of which John Lennon met his end).
After the Dialectics of Liberation conference
at the Roundhouse (more later), Panna threw
a party for everyone involved. Among others,
Mick Jagger was there and naturally it included
Burroughs, who appeared from upstairs when
the police were called following a fight between
poets. According to Miles, Burroughs told them:
'I can assure you that nothing ever happens at
Panna's house. Nothing at all. Good evening.'
And with that he promptly shut the door in
their faces.

**Retrace your steps to Outer Circle and
turn left and left again into Hanover Gate
with the mosque on your right. At Park**

Road, turn right, cross over the road and the Regent's Canal and at the roundabout keep ahead into Wellington Road with Lord's Cricket Ground on the left. Go left past the ground into Wellington Place and right into Cavendish Avenue.

Paul McCartney and Jane Asher owned the house at No. 7 on the left and this is where Ginsberg ended up following a reading at the Queen Elizabeth Hall on the South Bank on 12th July 1967. Mick Jagger and Marianne Faithfull also happened to be there that night and they discussed magic and mysticism.

Continue on Cavendish Avenue to Circus Road. If you want to take in the legendary Abbey Road Studios turn left and then right at Grove End Road which becomes Abbey Road. The studios are at No. 3 across the road - impossible to miss as they're covered in graffiti (this detour will add about half a mile and 15 minutes to the walk).

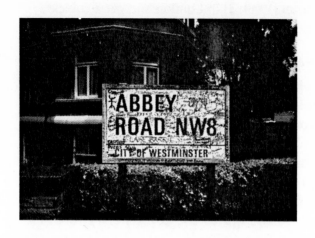

Otherwise, turn right on Circus Road, cross Wellington Road and on the left is Kingsmill Terrace.

On this street at No. 33 once stood a house where Kerouac's friend Seymour Wyse lived (probably on the site of St John's Car Park). In a letter to Ginsberg in 1957, he wrote:
'Dug all London too, including performance of St Matthew Passion in St Paul's Cathedral [Walk 4], and saw Seymour who is at 33 Kingsmill. Even Seymour dint put me up in London because of some cunt in there who hated me, I'm gettin to be like Burroughs. Seymour still slim and boyish but strangely unemotional, tho as we were strolling through Regent Park one evening he let out a shout of recognition. Go to the Mapleton

Hotel [Walk 3] in London and get a cubicle room, cheapest possible.'

Continue on Circus Road and at St John's Wood High Street it turns into St John's Wood Terrace. Go ahead to reach Townshend Road, turn right and then left on Allitsen Road, cross The Avenue and continue ahead down St Edmunds Terrace to the end, crossing Ormonde Terrace into Primrose Hill park. Turn left and climb the hill to the top where there is a magnificent view.

GURU

It is the moon that disappears
It is the stars that hide not I
It's the City that vanishes, I stay
with my forgotten shoes
my invisible stocking
It is the call of a bell

Primrose Hill May '65
Allen Ginsberg - Planet News (1968)

Primrose Hill was also the inspiration behind The Beatles' *The Fool on the Hill*. The event which prompted this song happened when Paul was walking his dog Martha, on the hill one morning. As he watched the sun rise, he noticed that Martha was missing. In an instant, Paul turned around to look for his dog, and there a man stood, who appeared on the hill without making a sound. The gentleman was dressed respectably, in a belted raincoat. Paul knew this man had not been there seconds earlier as he had looked in that direction for Martha. Paul and the stranger exchanged a greeting, and this man then spoke of what a beautiful view it was from the top of this hill that overlooked London. Within a few seconds, Paul looked around again, and the man was gone.

Passing the viewing platform and turn right heading downhill with Primrose Hill Road on the left. At the corner of the park Primrose Hill Road joins Regent's Park Road. Turn left and follow Regent's Park Road as it bends right to reach Gloucester Avenue with a footbridge over the railway directly ahead. Cross the bridge and turn right (still on Regent's Park Road) and on the right before the main road is the entrance to the Roundhouse.

This was formerly a railway engine turning shed and it became an arts venue in the 60s. The *Dialectics of Liberation* conference was held here on 27th July 1967. Organised by R D Laing, who was seeking to 'demystify human violence in all its form', Ginsberg was invited to give an address and produced *Consciousness and Practical Action*. Notably, he was rather disturbed by Gregory Bateson's introduction to the greenhouse effect theory. The conference was recorded and later released on a set of albums and a documentary on Ginsberg's visit was produced for German TV under the title *Ah! Sunflower*.

Earlier, on 11th October 1966, this was the venue for the launch of *International Times* (also known as *IT*). Yoko Ono and Paul McCartney attended, with Paul dressed as an Arab to avoid recognition and Balch's Towers Open Fire and *The Cut-Ups* were shown. Pink Floyd and Soft Machine (named after the Burroughs novel) played. Visiting poet Kenneth Rexroth (MC at the famous Six Gallery reading in San Francisco on 7th October 1955 which introduced Ginsberg, Snyder, Whalen, Lamantia and McClure to the world), somewhat taken aback by the music and worried about the fire risk, left early. Burroughs appeared in issues 2 and 3 of *IT*. The Beatles announced they would return to playing live here in 1968, but it never happened.

**Continue down to Chalk Farm Road
and turn left to find the tube station on
Adelaide Road. Take the City part of the
Northern Line (via Bank) and get off at
Old Street, which will take about 10/15
minutes. Take Exit 5 which will bring
you out on City Road and walk ahead up
to Bunhill Fields on your right, opposite
Wesley's Chapel.**

Bunhill Fields is a graveyard for nonconformist
burials, with many religious leaders such as John
Bunyan and founder of the Quakers George Fox,
also Daniel Defoe, author of Robinson Crusoe.
On your right past the little maintenance
building is a gravestone recording that William
Blake (1757-1827) lies nearby ('nearby' as Bunhill
Fields was bombed during World War II and
graves were scattered, though there are moves
to relocate the grave again so look for notices in
the window of the building).

Ginsberg and Corso were here in 1958 and in a letter to Gary Snyder from Paris, Corso wrote: 'I was in London and saw Blake's grave in Bunhill Center (sic). O that poetry were cannibalistic enough to eat the I.'

Once in a sublet apartment in East Harlem, Ginsberg, sitting on the bed, dipped into William Blake's Songs of Innocence and Experience. He heard a voice in the room which he knew, without having to ask how he knew, was the voice of Blake himself. The book was open at the 'Songs of Experience' poem:

AH, SUNFLOWER

Ah, sunflower, weary of time,
Who countest the steps of the sun;
Seeking after that sweet golden clime
Where the traveller's journey is done;

Where the Youth pined away with desire,
And the pale virgin shrouded in snow,
Arise from their graves, and aspire
Where my Sunflower wishes to go!

'I rushed up enchanted - it was my first
sunflower, memories of Blake - my visions -
Harlem'
(from Ginsberg's Sunflower Sutra).

Ginsberg also made recordings of Blake's Songs
of Innocence and Experience in 1969 and 1979.

**To find the Hand & Shears in Middle
Street (NB: closed at weekends), a pub
with lots of small rooms and a clientele of
City types and staff from Barts hospital
and Smithfield meat market, continue
straight ahead through Bunhill Fields
to Bunhill Row (the Artillery Arms is
opposite and is usually open all week),
turn left and then right into Chiswell
Street. Continue ahead at the crossroads
(with the King's Head on the corner) into**

Beech Street, which is now an underpass with the Barbican Arts Centre on your left. Cross Aldersgate Street (Barbican tube on the Circle and Metropolitan Lines is on the opposite corner) into Long Lane, turn immediately left into Cloth Street and then right into Middle Street. This will add another half mile and 15 minutes onto the walk.

Fitzrovia, Bloomsbury & Soho

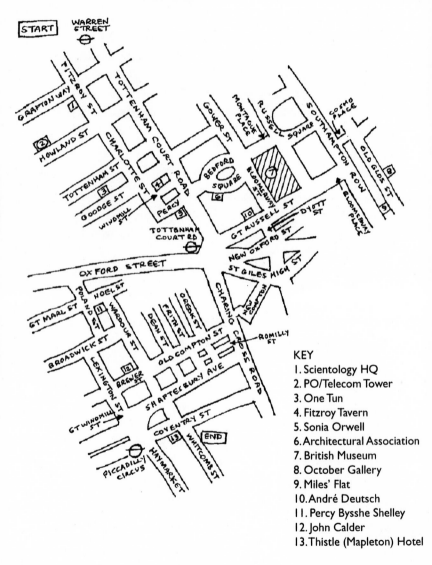

KEY
1. Scientology HQ
2. PO/Telecom Tower
3. One Tun
4. Fitzroy Tavern
5. Sonia Orwell
6. Architectural Association
7. British Museum
8. October Gallery
9. Miles' Flat
10. André Deutsch
11. Percy Bysshe Shelley
12. John Calder
13. Thistle (Mapleton) Hotel

Walk 3
Fitzrovia, Bloomsbury and Soho
3.5 Miles - 2-3 Hours

**From Warren Street tube on the Victoria
or Northern Line, turn right to walk down
Tottenham Court Road, then right into
Grafton Way and then left into Fitzroy
Street by the statue of Francisco De
Miranda.**

On the right at No. 37 Fitzroy Street was the HQ of Scientology and in 1967 Burroughs enrolled himself here onto the Beginners Course. Ted Morgan in *Literary Outlaw* records that for Ian Sommerville, this was the last straw. Burroughs was on an auditing binge and he wanted to round up people in the street and chain them to E-meters. When he tried to audit Ian, he fled, telling Miles, 'When Bill turns on the Operating Thetan glare on me, I just know it's time to leave.' Returning to Duke Street (Walk 4) on weekends, Burroughs used postcard photographs of L Ron Hubbard as targets for his air pistol. He eventually left Scientology, impressed by the auditing techniques but disgusted by the authoritarian organisation and the stupidly fascistic utterances of L Ron Hubbard. However, he did use Scientology texts in *The Cut-Ups*.

Continue straight on, cross Howland Street and pausing on the corner turn to look right to gaze up at the Telecom Tower (formerly the Post Office Tower).

In June 1965, Miles was with Corso, Ginsberg and Ferlinghetti when Corso suddenly saw the tower and yelled in an outraged voice to passing pedestrians: 'Hey! Who put that there?' I wonder if he knew that one of his favourite poets, Arthur

Rimbaud lived at Number 34 (now gone) with fellow poet Paul Verlaine, close to where the tower now stands, during the closing months of 1872 (however, a house where they lived still exists - Walk 2).

Continue on into Charlotte Street and cross Tottenham Street and Goodge Street.

There used to be a folk club in Finch's pub (now The One Tun) on Goodge Street in the 60s, where poetry was also performed. Ginsberg read for the 'resolutely working class' Peanuts group in 1965. The pub was the home of Donovan's 'violent hash smoker' who 'shook a chocolate machine' in his song Sunny Goodge Street. Donovan's *Beat Café* was released in 2004 and the cover says: 'In this new CD "Beat Café" Donovan explores the world of the bohemian café. The jazz and poetry, the folk and the blues, the philosophy and Buddhist meditation and the modern art lifestyle, all of which informed and influenced popular culture. Three writers emerged and defined the Beat Generation - Jack Kerouac, Allen Ginsberg and William Burroughs. The 40s and 50s saw these three form a trio of dynamism that opened the doors of freedom.' The CD includes a version of the Dylan Thomas poem Do Not Go Gentle.

Donovan toured with the album in 2005 and, in Oxford, folk singer Julie Felix accompanied him for a couple of numbers (Walk 5).

Continue further down and on the corner of Charlotte Street and Windmill Street is the Fitzroy Tavern.

David Archer's Parton Press was the first to publish Dylan Thomas, George Barker and David Gascoyne and in 1958 he introduced Ginsberg and Corso to Barker, who took them to the French pub, the Coach & Horses (both to come later in the walk), the Fitzroy Tavern and all the Soho and Fitzrovia pubs frequented by the London literary crowd. Lots of famous writers and artists drank here (there is a Writers & Artists' Bar downstairs), including George Orwell and Dylan Thomas (he met his wife Caitlin here in 1936).

Continue ahead and turn left into Percy Street (Sonia Brownell, later Sonia Orwell, lived on the right at No. 18 Percy Street - Walk 5) and stop on Tottenham Court Road.

Somewhere on Tottenham Court Road in the early 80s, Burroughs took part in a cameo role for a German underground movie called

Decoder. He played the proprietor of an electronics shop who dismantles a cassette recorder. Also filming through the shop window was notable film auteur, Derek Jarman, who used the footage for his film The Pirate Tape.

Now cross over and bear right into Bedford Square by the Jack Horner pub. Turn right and at No. 36 is The Architectural Association.

Following the Royal Albert Hall extravaganza, Ginsberg, Corso, Ferlinghetti and Andrei Voznesensky were recorded here in 1965 by Miles for an album release.

Continue around the square to reach the junction of Gower/Bloomsbury Street, turn left and then cross over to turn right into Montague Place. Walk past the back of the British Museum into Russell Square and bear right around the square to reach Southampton Row. Turn right and cross over to turn left into Cosmo Place and then by St George's church, turn right into Old Gloucester Street. At No. 24 on the left in Lundonia House is the October Gallery.

Burroughs had a solo exhibition here in 1988 and three joint exhibitions with Keith Haring from 1988-1990, which included his 'shotgun' paintings (painted on mylar and wood blocks and then blasted with a 12-gauge).

Return to Southampton Row and turn left (noting on the corner a blue plaque stating that Sir John Barbirolli 1899-1970 was born here - Kerouac's conductor in Walk 1) and stop outside No. 102, opposite Spink's.

The Indica Bookshop moved here from Mason's Yard (Walk 4) in June 1966 and Miles and Peter Asher (Jane Asher's brother) used the local Italian restaurants to discuss business ideas. Miles and his girlfriend Sue had also been fortunate to find a flat on the top floor at No. 100. International Times had its offices in the basement. Here, in December 1966, Burroughs did a cut up of one of the IT poster issues which featured one of his texts. He also put a card on the notice board offering free Scientology auditing sessions, which included his address and telephone number. Miles says that he left wishing everyone a Merry Christmas with no trace of a smile or goodwill on his sombre visage.

Continue on and cross Southampton Row again, turning right into Bloomsbury Place which leads into Great Russell Street. Walk down to the British Museum.

In a letter to poet Philip Whalen in April 1957, Kerouac wrote: 'Saw stupa sculpts in British Museum here, & also coat-of-arms of my old ancestral Brittany family with motto: AIMER, TRAVAILLER ET SOUFFRIR (précis of Town & City plot!).' He went on to use this in *Lonesome Traveler*: 'In the British Museum I looked up my family in *Rivista Araldica*, IV, Page 240, "Lebris de Keroack. Canada, originally from Brittany. Blue on a stripe of gold with three silver nails. Motto: Love, work and suffer." I could have known.' Ginsberg also visited in 1958 and wrote to Peter Orlovsky: 'Elgin Marbles Naked Love in British Museum. Greatest thing in Europe.'

Continue on Great Russell Street, crossing Bloomsbury Street and on the right is No. 105.

This used to be the premises of Andre Deutsch, Kerouac's UK publisher. On 3rd April 1957, having heard about the forthcoming publication of *On The Road*, he wrote from Tangier to his US agent Sterling Lord: 'Hallelujah, and I was just on my way to London to stay with a friend and wait for a job back on a merchant ship! I'll look up Mr Deutsch. *On the Road* might go over big in Rock & Roll hooligan England, just as it might in the USA & thank God it doesn't teach meanness, but SOUL.' However, in a following letter, dated 20th April, he writes: 'I didn't see Andre Deutsch, not much time, but it occurred to me maybe it would double the sales to change the title to ROCK AND ROLL ROAD or at least invent a similar subtitle. English immigration almost didn't let me through because they thought I was a tramp.' Thankfully Sterling Lord resisted the idea to change the title of On The Road.

Turn around and go right into Dyott Street, cross New Oxford Street, continue down Dyott Street and at the end turn right into St Giles High Street. Cross over to go left into New Compton Street.

Somewhere near the end, at Nos. 3, 4 and 5, once stood Better Books. In the late 50s and early 60s, this was probably the only place in London where City Lights and Grove Press books could be found. The manager was Bill Butler, a poet from Missoula, Montana who had his poems published in the short lived beat magazine *Beatitude*. He moved to Brighton in 1965 and started the equally well know Unicorn Bookshop. Miles took over as manager of the paperback shop, importing and selling copies of Henry Miller titles to the local dirty bookshops. Poets and writers were welcome (though not Alexander Trocchi as stock seemed to go missing whenever he was around!). Basil Bunting, the Northumbrian poet, who Ginsberg admired, launched his best known work *Briggflatts* here.

Ginsberg gave a reading at Better Books in 1965 which was sold out and fans stood outside to listen. In the audience was Andy Warhol accompanied by Edie Sedgwick and Gerard Malanga (who took a series of photos of Burroughs in London in the 70s) and Donovan. Ian Sommerville taped it and it was released as a limited edition of 99 copies as *Allen Ginsberg at Better Books*. Peter Whitehead recalls: 'I'd gone to a poetry reading at Better Books to listen to Allen Ginsberg, having read *Howl* at Cambridge. By midnight, stoned out of our minds, the poets and various followers decided to rent the Albert Hall, invite Corso, Ferlinghetti, Vosnesensky, Yevtushenko and William Burroughs. Philip Larkin was not on the list. Nor Stevie Smith. Only Americans could be so brash as to imagine they could fill the Albert Hall with worshippers of hitherto unheard Beat poetry.' (Walk 1). Ferlinghetti also did a reading here and it too was recorded and released in an edition of 99 copies (for tax reasons). It included a song with Julie Felix (Walk 5).

Allen Ginsberg reading at Better Books

At the end, turn right and then left down the alleyway into Charing Cross Road. Turn left and then right into Old Compton Street.

This is the heart of Soho. Kerouac describes his impressions from 1957 in *Desolation Angels*. 'I managed to borrow five pounds from my English agent at his home (Buckingham Gate) and hurried thru the Soho (Saturday Midnight) looking for a room. Soho is the Greenwich Village of London full of sad Greek and Italian restaurants with checkered tablecloths by candlelight, and jazz hangouts, nightclubs, strip joints and the like, with dozens of blondes and brunettes cruising for money. Teddy Boys are dandies on street corners (like our own brand of special zooty well-dressed or at least "sharp" hipsters with lapel-less jackets or soft Hollywood-Las Vegas sports shirts). The usual bearded Bohemians also roam around Soho but they've been there since well before Dowson or De Quincy.' Somewhere in Soho were Antony Balch's offices. Following his untimely death, musician and artist Genesis P-Orridge was alerted by Brion Gysin that 28 cans of his films were about to be dumped and he had to use his unemployment money to get over here in a taxi and rescue them.

Walking down Old Compton Street, you will cross Greek Street, Frith Street and finally Dean Street. On the left in Greek Street is the Coach & Horses and also on the left in Dean Street is the French

House, both drinking haunts of the Bohemian literary crowd of the 50s and 60s mentioned earlier. At Frith Street turn left and at No. 29 on the corner of Romilly Street once stood the Moka Bar.

This was London's first milk bar, opened by Gina Lollabrigida in 1953. It closed in 1973, but was it down to Burroughs? As Ted Morgan puts it: 'Burroughs began to feel he was in enemy territory. There was a Soho espresso joint, the Moka Bar, where on several occasions a snarling counterman had treated him with outrageous and unprovoked discourtesy. He decided to retaliate by putting a curse on the place. On August 3rd, 1973, he took pictures and made recordings, in plain sight of the horrible old proprietor. When the Moka Bar closed down on October 30th Burroughs was sure his curse had worked.' One of Burroughs' favourite restaurants, La Capannina, can still be found at 24 Romilly Street.

Return to Old Compton Street via Dean Street and cross over. On the right at No. 45, with a discreet sign, is The Groucho Club.

The Groucho Club is a private club opened in 1985 as 'the antidote to the traditional club'. It is named after Groucho Marx because of his famous remark about not joining any club that would have him as a member. Many members are drawn from the media, entertainment, arts and fashion industries including lots of writers. Ginsberg stayed here on his last visit to London in 1995 (Walk 4).

Return to Old Compton Street, turn right and at the end turn right again into Wardour Street, walk ahead and turn left into Broadwick Street, crossing Berwick Street and its market, to turn right into Poland Street. Just before the junction with Great Marlborough/Noel Street, at No. 15 on the left, there is a blue plaque to Percy Bysshe Shelley (1792-1822).

Shelley
by
gregory corso

In a letter to Allen Ginsberg in 1958, Corso wrote: 'Shelley leads me to a safe unreal high gold muse, and life leads the opposite.' Shelley was his undoubted hero and he had a 'love and a madness for Shelley'. *I Held a Shelley Manuscript* expresses his delight in holding his words in his hands:

I HELD A SHELLEY MANUSCRIPT

My hands did numb to beauty
as they reached into Death and tightened!

O sovereign was my touch
upon the tan-inks's fragile page!

Quickly, my eyes moved quickly,
sought for smell for dust for lace
for dry hair!

I would have taken the page
breathing in the crime!
For no evidence have I wrung from dreams—
yet what triumph is there in private credence?

Often, in some steep ancestral book
when I find myself entangled with leopard-apples
and torched-skin mushrooms
my cypressean skein outreaches the recorded age
and I, as though tipping a pitcher of milk,
pour secrecy upon the dying page.

Gregory Corso - The Happy Birthday of Death (1960)

Corso died on 17th January 2002. His ashes were taken to Rome and buried at the feet of Shelley.

William Blake (Walk 2) once lodged at No. 28 Poland Street and at the top is Oxford Street, where the Cinephone cinema used to be. Balch's *The Cut-Ups* premiered here in 1967 and was shown with *Towers Open Fire*. They ran for two weeks only as the staff couldn't stand running it five times a day and because of the disorientation caused to the patrons. Some loved it, some hated it. Members of the audience would rush out saying 'It's disgusting' and there was also an unusually high incidence of articles being left behind in the theatre!

Go back down Poland Street, cross Broadwick Street and bear right into Lexington Street by the John Snow pub. At the end is Brewer Street.

Opposite is the Vintage Magazine shop, handy for Beat articles in back issues of magazines like Esquire, Playboy or Rolling Stone.

Turn left and at No. 18, on the corner of Green's Court, used to be the office of John Calder, publishers, when they brought out Naked Lunch in 1964. They were also

UK agents for the Olympia Press at that time. Turn back and then left into Great Windmill Street and right on Shaftesbury Avenue towards Piccadilly Circus. Cross over Shaftesbury Avenue at the lights to stand opposite the statue of Eros, no doubt swarming with youngsters.

As a young merchant seaman during the war, Kerouac also naturally headed for Piccadilly Circus. He describes the night in Vanity of Dulouz: 'Me and the Four Quartets soldier, and the drinking soldier, bumped on down the road together straight for Piccadilly Circus bars and late Scotch. We got plowed and stupified in there till the very end when by God the host did actually yell out over the yells of airmen and soldiers "Hurry up please gentlemen it's time." We spilled out of there into the darkness of Piccadilly, fur coats of whores kept bumping up agin ye, "Ducks, I saye!" and "Hey, where?" I lost everybody and finally one fur coat said its name was "Lillian" and so we went off together into a cozy little inn.' Ferlinghetti was here during the war and in an interview from 1994 with Mike Plumbley, he describes what happened to him. 'I was the skipper of a US subchaser in the Normandy Invasion. We were battered by the storm that hit the beaches after the landings began, and limped back to England, partly under sail. We finally got one engine working and made it back to Southampton. (Some of the sailors jumped off and kissed the earth when we got back to the docks, having believed we were goners.) We were sent to a shipyard in Cowes and laid up for three weeks, most of which I spent in London.' No doubt, like all servicemen, he too spent some time in Piccadilly. As he says in a passage in his poem:

AUTOBIOGRAPHY

I landed in Normandy
in a rowboat that turned over
I have seen the educated armies
on the beach at Dover

Lawrence Ferlinghetti - A Coney Island of the Mind (1958)

Ginsberg and Corso in 1958 were broke, as usual, and one evening they found themselves hungry and penniless at midnight on Piccadilly. They had met the bookseller and publisher David Archer at a party and in desperation Allen telephoned him. He came and found Ginsberg and Corso, bought them a meal, and gave them a little money 'for poetry's sake'.

STUDYING THE SIGNS: AFTER READING RIGGFLATTS

White light's wet glaze on asphalt city floor,
the Guinness Time house clock hangs sky misty,
yellow Cathay food lamps blink, rain falls
on rose neon Swiss Watch under Regent archway,
Sun Alliance and London Insurance Group stands
granite – "Everybody gets torn down" . . . as a high
black taxi with orange doorlight passes around
iron railing blazoned with red sigma Underground –
Ah where the cars glide slowly round Eros
shooting down on one who stands in Empire's Hub
under his shining silver breast, look at Man's
sleepy face under half-spread metal wings –
Swan & Edgar's battlement walls the moving Circus,
princely high windows barred (shadow bank
interior office stairway marble) behind castiron
green balconies emblemed with single swans afloat
like white teacups what – Boots' blue sign lit up
over an enamel weight-machine's mirror clockface
at door betwixt plateglass Revlon & slimming bisquit
plaques and that alchemical blood-crimson pharmacy
bottle perched on street display. A Severed Head
"relished uproariously" above the masq'd Criterion
marquee, with Thespis and Ceres plaster Graces lifting
white arms in the shelled niches above a fire gong
on the wooden-pillard façade whose mansard gables
lean in blue-black sky drizzle, thin flagpole.
Like the prow of a Queen Mary the curved building
sign Players package, blue capped center
Navvy encircled by his life-belt a sweet bearded
profile against 19'th century sea waves –
last a giant red delicious Coca Cola signature
covers half the building back to gold Cathay.
Cars stop three abreast for the light, race forward,
turtleneck youths jump the fence toward Boots,

81

the night-gang in Mod slacks and ties sip
coffee at the Snac-A-Matic corner opendoor,
a boy leaned under Cartoon Cinema lifts hand
puffs white smoke and waits agaze – a wakened
pigeon flutters down from streetlamp to the fountain,
primly walks and pecks the empty pave – now deep
blue planet-light dawns in Piccadilly's low sky.

June 12, 1965

Allen Ginsberg - Planet News (1968)

Turn left into Coventry Street, passing the Haymarket.

Down here used to be the Icelandic Steakhouse (whatever one of those was) and also nearby were the Scandia Rooms in the Piccadilly Hotel. Apparently Burroughs used to frequent such places as he liked to sit in empty restaurants, where he could sit in the corner furthest away from the waiters.

Turn right opposite the Swiss Centre into Whitcomb Street.

The Thistle Hotel (actually No. 39 Coventry Street) used to be called The Mapleton. This is the cheap hotel Kerouac found in 1957 (though I suspect that is no longer the case) and he describes it thus in *Desolation Angels*. 'Piccadilly Circus, where I got my cheap hotel room,

Jack Kerouac
Scattered Poems

is the Times Square of London except there are charming street performers who dance and play and sing for pennies thrown at them, some of them sad violinists recalling the pathos of Dickens' London.' And in *Lonesome Traveler*. 'Finally I got a fifteen-bob room in the Mapleton Hotel (in the attic) and had a long divine sleep with the window open, in the morning the carillons blowing all of an hour round eleven and the maid bringing in a tray of toast, butter, marmalade, hot milk and a pot of coffee as I lay there amazed.' On 4th November 1963 the *With The Beatles* LP was cut at Abbey Road (Walk 2). There was an appearance on the Royal Command (Variety) Performance at the Prince of Wales Theatre and the BBC filmed it. Afterwards, the Beatles retired to the bar of the Mapleton Hotel.

If the drinking haunts of the French House at 49 Dean Street and the Coach & Horses at 29 Greek Street (see earlier) don't appeal, return to Coventry Street and head towards Piccadilly Circus (which is the nearest tube on the Piccadilly or Bakerloo Line). Turn left on Haymarket, cross over and go down Jermyn Street, cross Regent Street and opposite St James's church, turn left into Duke of York Street. At No. 2 is The Red Lion, with an amazing glass panelled and mirrored interior.

St Paul's to St James's

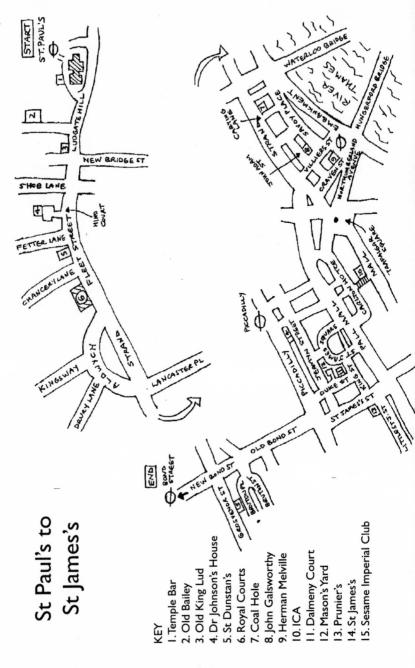

KEY
1. Temple Bar
2. Old Bailey
3. Old King Lud
4. Dr Johnson's House
5. St Dunstan's
6. Royal Courts
7. Coal Hole
8. John Galsworthy
9. Herman Melville
10. ICA
11. Dalmeny Court
12. Mason's Yard
13. Prunier's
14. St James's
15. Sesame Imperial Club

Walk 4
St Paul's to St James's
4.5 Miles - 2-3 Hours

Take Exit 2 from St Paul's tube station on the Central Line and turn left into Panyer Alley to the cathedral. Turn right and go around to the front and the main steps, noting the archway of Temple Bar on the right (Temple Bar used to divide the City from Westminster).

Kerouac in his brief 1957 stay describes his longing in *Lonesome Traveler*:

'And on a Good Friday afternoon a heavenly performance of the St Matthew Passion by the St Paul's choir. I cried most of the time and saw a vision of an angel in my mother's kitchen and longed to go home to sweet America again.'

A year later Ginsberg climbed up to the Whispering Gallery in the dome and looked out over London. The area surrounding St Paul's had been completely destroyed during the war and everywhere he could still see men clearing bomb sites and erecting new buildings.

Turn right to go down Ludgate Hill to Ludgate Circus, passing Old Bailey on your right with the dome of the court in the distance.

On the corner of Ludgate Circus once stood the Old King Lud public house and in 1957 Kerouac 'went into the King Lud pub for a sixpenny Welsh rarebit and a stout'. There is still a bust of the Old King below an iron lamp above the door.

Continue ahead into Fleet Street.

Kerouac in *Desolation Angels*: 'Fleet Street where by God I saw old 55-year-old Julian of the future a bowlegged blondy Scotsman emerging from the Glasgow Times tweaking his mustache, hurrying on twinkling newspaperman feet to the nearest pub, the King Lud, to foam at beers of Britain's barrels - Under the streetlamp right where Johnson and Boswell strolled, there he goes, in tweed suit.'

Passing Ye Olde Cheshire Cheese pub, turn right into Hinde Court and follow the signs to Gough Square to see first a statute of Hodge the cat ('a very fine cat indeed') and then the house of the great lexicographer and lover of London life, Dr Johnson.

He lived here from 1749-59 and in a letter to his friend Ed White, dated 28th April 1957 and sent from New York, Kerouac writes: 'Wanted to write you from Dr Johnson's house in London when I was there but got too engrossed in the British Museum and staring at El Grecos in the National Gallery.'

Return to Fleet Street and continue on to pass St Dunstan's with the statues of Gog and Magog on the belfry to reach the City Griffin (where Temple Bar once stood) and onto the Strand. Continue on with the Royal Courts of Justice on your right and in an island in the road is St Clement Danes church.

Outside the church is a statue of Dr Johnson on a plinth as he used to worship here. The plinth also features two bas-reliefs of Dr Johnson with Boswell and with Mrs Thrale.

Go round the semi-circular Aldwych, passing Kingsway and Drury Lane to reach Waterloo Bridge. Cross over at the junction and gaze across the river to the South Bank complex.

On 12th July 1967, Ginsberg gave a reading there at the Queen Elizabeth Hall with Charles Olson, W H Auden, Stephen Spender and the Italian poet Giuseppe Ungaretti.

Continue along the Strand to the Savoy Hotel.

Linda and Paul McCartney held a reception here following their wedding on 12th March 1969.

Turn left down Carting Lane by the Coal Hole pub to the back of the hotel. Turn right on Savoy Place and on the next right is an enclosed alley.

Here, on 8th May 1965, Bob Dylan made his promotional film for his latest single, *Subterranean Homesick Blues*. It was used as the opening sequence for D A Pennebaker's film *Don't Look Back*. Dylan holds up placards (handwritten by Ginsberg and Donovan in the hotel) with key words from the song and casts them aside as the song unfolds. In the background with musician Bob Neuwirth and holding a long stick is Ginsberg. Pennebaker says of Dylan:

'He was very assured of who he was, but he was actually kind of inventing himself as he went along. He was like a person who had just stepped out of a Kerouac book.'

Dylan and Ginsberg visited Kerouac's grave on the Rolling Thunder tour in 1975.

Just past the alley on Savoy Place are some steps which lead up to Adephi Terrace. Climb up and go ahead on the terrace, following it round into Robert Street. A blue plaque on the left at Nos.1-3 identifies the house of John Galsworthy (1867-1933).

On his way to England in 1943, Kerouac writes in *Vanity of Duluoz*: 'In my bunk I read, of all things, the entire Galsworthy *Forsythe Saga*, which not only gives me a view of British life before I get there, but gives me an idea about sagas, or legends, novels connecting into one grand tale.' This became what he called 'The

Duluoz Legend', which can be pieced together in sequence from Kerouac's novels.

Continue on to John Adam Street and turn left, then at Villiers Street at the end, turn left and then right under the arches into Craven Passage.

Here is the well known gay venue, Heaven, where Ginsberg gave a reading as a guest of the Megatripolis Club on 19th October 1995. This was released on DVD as *Allen Ginsberg - Live in London* in 2005 by Diva Pictures.

Continue through and up the steps past the double pub, The Ship & Shovel, and turn left into Craven Street to reach No. 25 and a new blue plaque for Herman Melville (1819-1891), who lived here in 1849.

Moby Dick; or, The Whale could be claimed as the 19th Century's equivalent of *On The Road* ('On The Sea?'). Kerouac called Neal Cassady, hero of *On The Road*, 'that mad Ahab at the wheel'.

Turn around and passing a brown plaque on the left at No. 35 where US President Benjamin Franklin (1706-1790) lived, return to the Strand and turn left to reach Trafalgar Square.

Kerouac in 1943 (*Vanity of Duluoz*): 'wanted to see pigeons, Trafalgar's statue of Nelson for some reason'.

HOW ONE LOOKS AT IT

Ah tricky cartographer, the map I follow
    ends where it begins.
Like the touching of the snow
    Athens was no longer Athens.
Must one keep home to keep Rome Rome?
Surely then this England visit
will spoil whatever dream I have of it.
O sneaky mighty real, you
deny me Horsa exclaiming hoar
    in his Aylesfordian tent, you
give me but thin accusations to scream:
the nation is dying
the lions are ravaging the unicorns
and Nelson's one eye is crying.

Gregory Corso - Selected Poems (1962)

Continue ahead, crossing Whitehall, to go through Admiralty Arch into the Mall. Walk up to the Institute of Contemporary Art (ICA) building on your right.

Burroughs performed twice here, in 1963 and
1965 and Ginsberg read here with his father
Louis, also a published poet, in 1967. The
Burroughs event of 1965 was a multimedia
experiment, in which Brion Gysin created and
then destroyed a six-foot-by-nine-foot painting
while Burroughs sat on stage in his hat and
Chesterfield overcoat, bathed in deep blue light,
reading from newspaper clippings and staring
fixedly at the audience. Daevid Allen (later of
The Soft Machine) also took part. The Ginsbergs
at the ICA was recorded and released on Saga
Records.

**Go up the side of the ICA via steps to
Carlton House Terrace, turn left and
then right into Carlton Gardens by the
statue of George Nathanial Curzon and
up to Pall Mall. Cross over into St James's
Square, turn left and right and then left
again in King Street and finally right into**

Duke Street St James's. On the right at No. 8 is Dalmeny Court.

Burroughs lived here off and on in Flat 22 from 1966-74. As well as the usual tape experiments, *The Wild Boys, The Last Words of Dutch Schultz, The Job, Port of Saints* and *Exterminator!* were all written here. It is said that when Ian Sommerville moved in here, he found Burrough's filing cabinet contained 5 labelled folders and 17 folders marked 'miscellaneous'. Burroughs received word of the death of Kerouac here on 22nd October 1969.

J G Ballard first met him here:
'This was in a street called Duke Street, literally about 100 yards from Piccadilly Circus. And, of course, this was of interest to him because that's where all the boys used to congregate, in the lavatory of the big Piccadilly Circus Underground station. They had completely taken it over. It was quite a shock for a heterosexual like myself to accidentally stray into this lavatory and to find oneself in what seemed to be a kind of oriental male brothel. He obviously found that absolutely fascinating.' At a dinner with Andy Warhol in 1980, Burroughs was asked by Victor Bockris about English sexuality and he recalled: 'They like to be beaten with rulers and hairbrushes. I've known boys who told me about various

practices. There was the egg man who had to be pelted with eggs for some reason. There was another man who made boys get into a big cage. He had a big birdcage and he would throw some bread in there and say, "Eat it!"'

Ted Morgan describes the atmosphere in 1966: 'Burroughs moved into a flat in Antony Balch's building, at 8 Duke Street. Ian [Sommerville] and Alan [Watson] were broke and in August asked if they could move in. They were like an old married couple, either bickering or silent. Ian complained that Burroughs was a creature of habit. He had to have his first drink at six, and then he was drunk by eight. He occasionally went to Sonia Orwell's, where he once ran into Stephen Spender. He also went to the home of Panna Grady, who had moved to London with the poet Charles Olson. Burroughs sometimes received admirers - David Bowie told him that his songs owed a lot to the cut-up method. Mick Jagger invited him to his wedding to Bianca and in May 1971, there was a flurry of activity over a film version of Naked Lunch. Jagger was interested, but when he came to the Duke Street flat, Burroughs could see it wasn't going to work. Mick did not want Balch as director. He didn't like him. He thought Balch was coming on to him sexually.

Genesis P-Orridge also has a tale to tell of Duke Street:

'In 1972 I was given a copy of File magazine from Toronto. I was looking through it and noticed William S. Burroughs, Duke Street, St.James - I thought, "Oh, he won't still be at this address, but still I'll send something anyway," and so I sent him a small booklet of about 30 pages with each page was hand drawn calligraphic collages, and it was called 'To do with smooth paper.' I was really shocked a week later, I got a postcard back, which said "Thank you for the smooth paper, William S. Burroughs." Shock, horror and excitement all at once - "Wow, he really exists, and he writes back too." So then I sent him a shoe box with a wax cast of Donovan's left hand minus the thumb. I sent him that with 'Dead Fingers Thumb' written on the box, and he liked that too. And then, just after that, I was moving to London - I had a friend who I stayed with and I gave that phone number to Burroughs in a letter. He rang up and said to this guy, "Hi there, this is William S. Burroughs here, I wanna talk to Genesis P-Orridge," and he said, "Oh sure, piss off," and put the phone down. When I came down to London a couple of weeks later, he said, "Some stupid bloke rang up pretending to be William Burroughs, so I just put the phone down on him," and I said, "Oh that probably was him, he's got this number". He says, "Oh shit! And I've always wanted to meet him and talk to him, and the one chance I get I go and put the phone down on him." So I sent yet another letter to Burroughs saying "now, what was the phone call about etc," and it was arranged that I should come to London, ring up from the railway station and he would pay for a taxi cab for me to go round to his flat to meet him. Which was what I did. That was in 1973.'

At the end of his time here, Burroughs was growing tired of London. He probably agreed with Anthony Burgess (author of *Clockwork Orange* with whom he frequented many London pubs), when Burroughs asked him if he saw many other writers in London, he replied, 'No, they're all a bunch of swine.' In an interview with Victor Bockris, he was asked if at any point he was close to the mythical swinging London scene and Burroughs replied: 'No not at all. It was going on,

I wasn't involved in at except very moderately, it didn't interest me much. So called "swinging London" seemed to occur when London, to my way of thinking, was very much on a downgrade, and I always wondered where is this swinging London?' At the age of fifty-nine, Burroughs was at the point of a crisis, certain that he had to leave England. Prices had doubled and the whole island was going downhill. His view of the English was not very complimentary: 'Just as Pavlov's dogs salivated at the bell, that happy breed grovel in front of the Queen, indulging in that debased, degraded and downright disgusting English custom of "knowing one's place", a custom enforced by an army of shopkeepers, waiters, hotel clerks and doormen.' Guy Fawkes had the right idea - 'blow the whole shithouse sky-high.'

It would be great to have a blue plaque put up here for Burroughs, but the rules are 100 years after birth or 25 years after death, so I guess we'll have to wait until 2014.

Further up Duke Street on the right is an alleyway which leads into Mason's Yard.

No. 6 in the far corner was the original home of the Indica Bookshop & Gallery and the gallery remained here when the bookshop moved to

Southampton Row (Walk 3). The three original owners were Barry Miles, John Dunbar and Peter Asher. Paul McCartney put up some money for the venture as well designing the wrapping paper and allowing his driver, Taffy, to use his Aston Martin to run errands for them. Ian Sommerville worked on the electrics and Burroughs used to drop by. In the early days, one frequent visitor was a teenage male model called Mark Feld, who later changed his name to Marc Bolan. It was here in 1966 (when it was just a gallery) that Yoko Ono had an exhibition, Unfinished Paintings and Objects and where she first met John Lennon.

Return to Duke Street and turn right at King Street, then left at St James's Street and walk down, passing Lock & Co the hatters and on the left just inside Pickering Place is a brass plaque. This is where the Texas Legation had their offices, when Texas was a Republic, from 1842-1845. On the other side on the corner of Little St James's Street, Nos.72-73 St James's Street once housed a famous old fish restaurant called Prunier's (currently Luciano).

Douglas Lyne recalls a conversation regarding
a brief encounter between Burroughs and his
nephew, Simon Seligman:
'My nephew heard that Burroughs was in town
and asked if I could get him an introduction. I
said that I thought he was unlikely to remember
me but why not go and see him anyway. He
went to his flat in Duke Street and was informed
that he was across the road at Prunier's. Simon
went there and said to Burroughs that he
thought he might know his uncle. Burroughs
said he never heard of me whereupon Simon
apologised and was about to leave, but
Burroughs said "Sit down and eat as you're here
anyway." He was always very open like that,
interested in whoever happened to be around.'
I like to think that Burroughs might have
smoked his odd looking cigarettes here. As

Miles recalls:

'A bottle of tincture of cannabis could be obtained on the National Health when prescribed by a doctor. Burroughs got his from Dr Dunbar and used to dip his Senior Service into the liquid, allow the cigarettes to dry, then put them back into the pack. The problem was that the cigarettes were all stained an eye-catching green and certainly smelled like pot when smoked. Burroughs insisted that no one ever noticed that they were not regular cigarettes when he lit up in a restaurant.' As he says, 'They were prescribed as a cure for paranoia - dope smokers were paranoid about being busted.'

Turn back up St James's Street and then turn right into Jermyn Street, home of expensive tailors and cigar stores.

On the right at No. 93 is Paxton & Whitfield, who have sold cheese here since 1797. One of the flats above the shop was the last London address of Aleister Crowley before his retirement to Hastings in 1945. Although a notorious drug fiend and Satanist, he was not particularly well liked by Burroughs. He thought that his well known dictum, 'Do what thou wilt is the whole of the Law' was plagiarised from Hassan-i-Sabbah's 'Nothing is true, everything is permitted' (Walk 1). Following an article on the Beats in *Life* magazine in November 1959,

Burroughs wrote to his mother hoping that he would not be ludicrously miscast and given the title (vacated by Aleister Crowley) as the wickedest man alive!

Turn left past St James Church into Piccadilly.

In 1998, on the day before Ferlinghetti took part in the Celebration of Kenneth Patchen at The Tate (Walk 5), he also read here at *A Celebration of the Life and Work of Allen Ginsberg* with other poets and writers including Anne Waldman, Tom Pickard, Adrian Mitchell, Michael Horovitz and Barry Miles. This is a fine church with lots of history and Ginsberg would have liked the connection with William Blake (Walk 2), who was baptised here in 1757.

Turn back on Piccadilly and cross over at the lights to turn right into Old Bond Street. Continue ahead past Bruton Street on to New Bond Street and then turn left into Grosvenor Street. Go over Davies Street and on the left at the house at No. 49 Grosvenor Street was once the home of the Sesame Imperial Club.

Edith Sitwell was a member and in 1958, she invited Ginsberg and Corso to dine with her.

She wore a long satin dress and a tall conical hat, like a character in a Book of Hours. Allen told Lucien [Carr], 'Lunch with Edith Sitwell in big expensive Lady Macbeth club - potted shrimps Roastbeef & treacle tart.' She told them she liked their work and that they were the hope of English-language poetry. Flattered Allen asked, 'May we own you?' and she held up her hand, palm uppermost, in regal gesture of acquiescence. Corso's version in a letter to poet LeRoi Jones goes: 'Saw Sitwell too - she invited us to lunch at her "club" - the Lady Macbeth Society - it was all very strange. Allen and I went to see her high. She ordered some very odd food for us, shrimps caught in frozen butter. She is real soul. Likes our poetry and when we offered to turn her on she gracefully declined saying "I fear I have been denied the joys of drugs - I once had morphine and became ill."

Further on is Grosvenor Square, home of the US Embassy, scene of anti-Vietnam riots in the 60s, but for the pub turn back and then right into Davies Street (for the tube turn left and walk up to Oxford Street to Bond Street station on the Central and Jubilee Lines), left in Berkeley Square and once more left into Bruton Place. In this typical London mews is The Guinea (closed Saturday afternoon and

Sunday), which would have once been the haunt of coachmen and servants and now has a reputation for fine steaks and equally fine beer. Alternatively, continue on down the side of Berkeley Square and turn right into Charles Street and at the end in Waverton Street is The Red Lion, another fine pub, which is open on Saturday and Sunday evenings and Sunday lunchtime. Pub diversions will add another quarter or half a mile (5-10 minutes) to the walk.

South West London

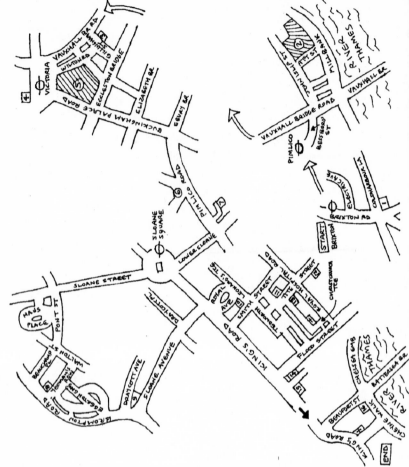

KEY
1. Ritzy Cinema
2. Tate Britain
3. Joseph Conrad
4. Shakespeare Pub
5. Victoria Station
6. Mozart
7. Dove Walk
8. Bunch of Grapes
9. Michelin Building
10. Bram Stoker
11. Mark Twain
12. Oscar Wilde
13. The Surprise
14. Chelsea Manor
    Studios
15. Chelsea Town Hall
16. Lindsey House

Walk 5
South West London
6 Miles - 3-4 Hours

This walk begins at the Ritzy cinema in Brixton.
From Brixton tube station on the Victoria Line,
exit onto Brixton Road and turn left, crossing
Electric Avenue to reach the cinema on the
corner of Coldharbour Lane.

Here, in four days from 29th September to 2nd
October 1982, Burroughs took part in an event
called The Final Academy. Organised by David
Dawson, Roger Ely and Genesis P-Orridge, there
were readings from the man himself and from
other long time collaborators, Brion Gysin, John
Giorno and Jeff Nuttall. There was also music

and other 'performances' from individuals such as Ian Hinchliffe (billed as an 'Absurdist') and bands like Cabaret Voltaire and Genesis' new outfit, Psychic TV. Antony Balch's films *Towers Open Fire, Cut-Ups, William Buys a Parrot* and *Bill and Tony* were also screened. A supporting exhibition was held at the B2 Gallery in Wapping Wall in the East End and an illustrated catalogue was produced.

Return to Brixton tube and take the Victoria Line to Pimlico. From Pimlico tube station on the Victoria Line, go ahead and bear left on Bessborough Street to reach Vauxhall Bridge Road. Cross at the lights and turn right, then left into John Islip Street, cross Ponsonby Place and turn right into Atterburg Street with the statue of Millais on the corner to reach the Tate Britain gallery.

Tate Britain has a separate wing devoted to J M W Turner and Corso in 1958 wrote to artist Robert LaVigne: 'Saw a lot of great Turners in England, he really was a prophetic painter.' The last of the Beat writers to visit London was Ferlinghetti in 1998 and on 18th May he took part in *Word, Image & Rhythms: A Celebration of Kenneth Patchen* (the poet) here.

From the Tate go back to Vauxhall Bridge Road and walk all the way up to Victoria, passing the tower of St James The Less (which has a rich ornate interior) and crossing Warwick Way/Rochester Row. (A third of a mile and twenty minutes can be cut off the walk by taking the tube to Victoria). On the left in Gillingham Street, at No. 17, there is a blue plaque at the former residence of Joseph Conrad (1857-1924).

In an interview with Victor Bockris, when asked: 'Who else do you read?', Burroughs replied: 'A writer who I read and reread constantly is Conrad. I've read practically all of him. He has somewhat the same gift of transmutation that Genet does. Genet is talking about people who are very commonplace and dull. The same with Conrad. He's not dealing with unusual people at all, but it's his vision of them that transmutes them. His novels are very carefully written.'

At the top of Vauxhall Bridge Road, turn left crossing Wilton Road to the station and the bus stands. Continue ahead and look out for The Shakespeare pub on the corner of Buckingham Palace Road.

In 1957 Kerouac was not too enamoured of the place as recalled in *Lonesome Traveler*:
'I arrive in London in the evening, Victoria Station, and go at once to a bar called "Shakespeare". But I might as well've walked into Schrafft's - white table cloths, quiet clinking bartenders, oak paneling among Stout ads, waiters in tuxedos, ugh, I walk out of there as fast as I can and go roaming in the night-time streets of London.'
Somewhere nearby was Hazel Guggenheim McKinley's flat. Hazel was Peggy Guggenheim's sister and Douglas Lyne recalls a typical evening there in 1965.
'There was a reception following an exhibition of paintings by Hazel in her mansion flat. She was furious after what she thought was insufficient appreciation of her gift to Ginsberg of six bottles of red wine in a galvanized iron bucket. She tore up the copy of Howl which he had signed for her, which I later recovered.'

I now have this rather unique copy!

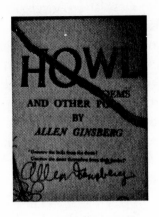

Turn left and walk down Buckingham
Palace Road, passing the coach station,
and cross at the lights opposite the police
station to turn right into Pimlico Road.
Walk along as it bends left passing antique
shops, the Orange Brewery pub and the
statue of Mozart in the little shady square.
On the left, just before **Lower Sloane
Street** is Dove Walk. Down this mews
at No. 3 is Christopher Gibbs antique
shop (who we will meet again). **At Lower
Sloane Street, turn right and walk up
to Sloane Square with the Royal Court
theatre on the right.**

Chelsea begins here and Kerouac's school friend
Seymour Wyse once had a record shop in
Chelsea (Ginsberg and Kerouac both stayed with

him - Walk 2). In Desolation Angels, Kerouac describes Chelsea a year earlier in 1957: 'As I walked thru the fogs of Chelsea looking for fish n chips a bobby walked in front of me half a block, just vaguely I could see his back and the tall bobby hat, and the shuddering poem occurred to me: "Who will strangle the bobby in the fog?" (for some reason I don't know, just because it was foggy and his back was turned to me and my shoes were silent and soft soled desert boots like the shoes of footpads).' Corso also went for the English fog:

NATURE'S GENTLEMAN

My first English fog!
And come at the right time
A terrible night in which I cursed
gentlemanliness
Out into it and ho the detective's hollow walk
Mary Dare? Art Thou Mary Dare?
And banged straight into a tree
and said Excuse Me

Gregory Corso - Long Live Man (1962)

Peter Davies, on whom J M Barrie based Peter Pan (Walk 1), threw himself under a tube train in Sloane Square station in 1960.

**Cross the square and walk ahead up
Sloane Street and just past the gardens
(private), turn left into Pont Street. The
World Psychedelic Centre operated in
a flat on Pont Street for a brief three
months in 1965-66.**

When set up by Michael Hollingshead, LSD
was still legal in the UK. Among visitors to the
centre were the usual suspects - Burroughs,
Sommerville, Trocchi, McCartney, R D Laing
and also Roman Polanski and Sharon Tate. On
the board was a certain old Etonian called
Christopher Gibbs. The police closed it down
in January 1966, arresting Hollingshead for
possession of hashish and he also ended up
doing time in Wormwood Scrubs (Walk 1).

**On the corner of Pont Street and Hans
Place, look out for a small blue plaque,
which records the fact that Jane Austen
stayed with her brother Henry in a
house on this site in 1814-15. At the
end, continue ahead into up market
Beauchamp Place and then turn left onto
Brompton Road. Turn left again by the
Bunch of Grapes pub into Yeoman's Row
and then right into Egerton Gardens.**

Burroughs stayed at No. 44 on the left while taking the Dent cure in 1956 (Walk 1).

Continue on as it bends left, then at the end, turn right to emerge back on Brompton Road. Turn left and at the Michelin building turn then left again into Sloane Avenue. Follow this all the way down to the King's Road and just before the junction with Draycott Place, at No. 7, there is a plaque to George Seferis (1900-1971), the Greek poet, ambassador and Nobel prize winner. Continue ahead into Anderson Street to King's Road, turn right and cross over. Stop at Wellington Square.

One of Kerouac's literary heroes, Thomas Wolfe, lived at No. 32 in 1926 while writing *Look Homeward Angel*. Kerouac's first novel, *The Town and the City*, is written in a style that owes a great deal to Wolfe.

Turn around and go right into Royal Avenue. At Leonard's Terrace, turn right and on your right at No. 18 is a blue plaque to Bram Stoker (1847-1912), author of *Dracula***.**

In Kerouac's *The Origin of the Beat Generation*, published in *Playboy* in June 1959, he says that it goes back to:

'That wild eager picture of me on the cover of
On the Road where I look so Beat goes back
much further than 1948 when John Clellon
Holmes (author of Go and The Horn) and I were
sitting around trying to think up the meaning
of the Lost Generation and the subsequent
Existentialism and I said "You know, this is really
a beat generation" and he leapt up and said
"That's it, that's right!"'

'...It goes back to the inky ditties of old cartoons
(Krazy Kat with the irrational brick) -- to
Laurel and Hardy in the Foreign Legion -- to
Count Dracula and his smile to Count Dracula
shivering and hissing back before the cross
-- to the Golem horrifying the persecutors
of the Ghetto -- to the quiet sage in a movie
about India, unconcerned about the plot-- to
the giggling old Tao Chinaman trotting down
the sidewalk of old Clark Gable Shanghai -- to
the holy old Arab warning the hotbloods that
Ramadan is near...'

'....To the Werewolf of London a distinguished
doctor in his velour smoking jacket smoking his
pipe over a lamplit tome on botany and suddenly
hairs grown on his hands, his cat hisses and he
slips out into the night with a cape and a slanty
cap like the caps of people in breadlines...'

Cross Smith Street into Tedworth Street and then turn left into Tedworth Square. Continue around and on the corner at No. 23 Tedworth Square, just before Tite Street, there is a blue plaque to Mark Twain (1835-1910), who lived here from 1896-97.

Could *The Adventures of Huckleberry Finn* by Samuel Langhorne Clemens be another claimant to the 19th Century version of *On The Road*?

'But I reckon I got to light out for the Territory ahead of the rest, because Aunt Sally she's going to adopt me and sivilize me, and I can't stand it. I been there before.'

Turn left into Tite Street and walk down, crossing Royal Hospital Road, to No. 34 on the right, where there is another blue plaque, this time for Oscar Wilde (1854-1900).

Corso wrote in a letter to James Laughlin in 1961:
'There's a publisher here wants to do all my books in one - Vestal Lady, Gasoline, Happy, and the new one [Selected Poems, Eyre & Spottiswoode, 1962]. I live on Oscar Wilde's street, Tite Street. London is wonderful, a relief after two years of alien tongues.'
In Anselm Hollo's poem, *Gregorio The Herald*, he describes the 'walls of his London room, covered with pictures of heroes - Rimbaud, Baudelaire, Poe'.

Go back up Tite Street and turn left into Christchurch Street and ahead is The Surprise pub.

Douglas Lyne recalls his meetings with Burroughs in The Surprise. 'The first time he came, he borrowed £1 off me. He then went off to Tangier and I received a sort of Christmas Card from him in December 1963 (the card is a hand painted desert scene) and a copy of a magazine, *My Own Mag*, he produced with Jeff

Nuttall which he described on a note on the cover as "an experiment in do it yourself present time writing", this was signed "Cordially William Burroughs". The last time I saw him he came to The Surprise to return my £1 and I asked him if I could interview him on tape, together with a friend of mine Henry Cohen (aka Roland Camberton, winner of the inaugural Somerset Maugham Prize for *Scamp* in 1951). Henry didn't like Burroughs much and only agreed reluctantly. We went across to my house at Number 1 Tite Street. I was a bit nervous and we had another friend acting as a technician and it was all a bit like Beckett's *Krapp's Last Tape* (play synopsis: "The past hopes and guilts of various characters return to mock and disquiet them as they near or pass the threshold of death"). The strained atmosphere meant that I ended up having a coughing fit with Burroughs suggesting all kinds of remedies. Still, I did make a tape of about 40 minutes, which I still have.'

Anselm Hollo also relates a story about Corso in a Chelsea pub in 1965:
'This may or may not have been after an evening at Beyond the Fringe, where we met Cyril Connolly, Peter Cook, and Dudley Moore - can't remember anything of consequence about that - and then proceeded to a Chelsea pub where Gregory was rebuffed by a young woman at the

bar and stormed out, inveighing against "English cunts". We then reeled down the street to a small Indonesian restaurant, ordered and ate some incredibly hot food, and had more drinkies. Gregory was still ranting about the inability of English girls to perceive him as their saviour, liberally lacing his sentences with "fucks", "shits" and "cunts", until a seven-foot Guardsman type (in civvies) appeared next to our table and sternly objected to such language, telling us that he had been enjoying a quiet dinner with a lady, etc., and offering to remove Gregory bodily from the premises if he didn't shut up pronto. Gregory then wanted to know if the Guardsman wanted to kill him and told him that if that was the case, he should please just go right ahead and do it. Two Bobbies then appeared on the scene with their classic "What seems to be the problem?" I told them Gregory was a renowned American poet, of a stature comparable to that of Dylan Thomas in the British Isles (come to think of it, perhaps not the best reference), and with Solomonic wisdom, the Bobbies decided that it was time for everyone to settle their reckonings and retire.'

Walk down Christchurch Terrace past the church and straight ahead into Flood Street. Turn right and at the top of the street on the left are Chelsea Manor Studios.

On 30th March 1967 in Michael Cooper's studio, this is where the cover for The Beatles album, *Sgt Pepper* was shot. Amongst others, Aleister Crowley (Walk 4), Bob Dylan (Walks 2 & 4), Dylan Thomas (Walk 2), H G Wells (Walk 2), Oscar Wilde (Walk 5) and Burroughs are all on the cover.

On the King's Road again, turn left, passing the Town Hall and just past, in between a row of shops at No. 189, is the entrance to King's Court North.

In 1965, Ferlinghetti was staying here in folk singer Julie Felix's flat in King's Court North and a party was held here after the International Poetry Incantation (Walk 1). Corso (being Corso) attacked both Ferlinghetti and Ginsberg for 'letting down the ideals of the Beat Generation', which they took with the usual pinch of salt.

Continue on crossing Oakley Street and on the other side of the road is Manresa Road.

Dylan and Caitlin Thomas (Walks 2 & 3), lived here during the war in 1942.

Continue on over Old Church Street and turn left into Beaufort Street, then right before reaching Battersea Bridge. On the corner of Cheyne Walk at Nos. 96-100 is an old large mansion house, known as Lindsey House.

There is a blue plaque to James McNeill Whistler (1834-1903), the American painter, at No. 96. This is where he painted the famous picture of his mother (Arrangement in Grey and Black: Portrait of the Painter's Mother, 1871) Also in this house, in a flat at No. 100 with the eagles on the doorposts, lived Christopher Gibbs. In the 60s, he was known as 'The King of Chelsea'. The original unpublished photograph, used on the cover of this book, was probably taken with Burroughs own camera in this flat. Burroughs' hat is perched next to him on a Roman torso of Apollo and his tape recorder can be seen on a table in the corner. Ian Sommerville, who installed a sound system for Gibbs, is standing behind him in the bay window passing what looks like a joint to Mikey Portman. Antonioni filmed parts of Blow-Up (1966) in Cheyne Walk and, apparently, some of the sex scenes took place here.

Standing back on the narrow pavement (be careful on this busy road!), a stone plaque can be seen above the doorway. It records that the original house was built in 1674 and was reconstructed in 1752 by Count Zinzendorf as the London headquarters of The Moravian Brethren.

Continuing along Cheyne Walk and turning left into Milman's Street leads pilgrims to the Moravian church and burial ground (though this is not usually open to the public) and back to the King's Road. Turn left and in a few minutes, appropriately enough, is The World's End pub, the end of our journey. From here it's a 20 minute walk back to Sloane Square tube station (or a No. 11 or 22 bus is quicker). However, as this part of London has changed a great deal since the 60s, so have the pubs and a return to The Surprise is worth the effort. It has an unusual Chelsea frieze and possibly even a Chelsea Pensioner or two from the Royal Hospital in their uniforms. An alternative

more pleasant route is to go back to
Cheyne Walk, to turn left past Albert
Bridge, left into Flood Street (which is just
before Chelsea Physic Garden founded in
1673 and open on Wednesday and Sunday
afternoons) and right into Christchurch
Street.

Bibliography

William Blake: Songs of Experience (William
    Blake, London, 1794)
Victor Bockris: With William Burroughs: A
    Report From The Bunker (Vermilion & Co,
    London, 1981)
Basil Bunting: Briggflatts (Fulcrum Press, London,
    1966)
William S Burroughs: The Naked Lunch (Olympia
    Press, Paris, 1959)
William S Burroughs: The Soft Machine (Olympia
    Press, Paris, 1961)
William S Burroughs: Ah Pook Is Here and
    Other Texts (John Calder, London, 1979)
William S Burroughs: Cities of the Red Night
    (Holt, Rinehart & Winston, New York, 1981)
William S Burroughs: A William Burroughs
    Reader (Pan Books, London, 1982)
William S Burroughs et al: The Final Academy:
    Statements of a Kind (The Final Academy,
    London, 1982)
William S Burroughs: The Adding Machine -
    Selected Essays (Seaver Books, New York,
    1986)
William S Burroughs: The Letters of William S
    Burroughs 1945 To 1959 (Viking Penguin,
    New York, 1993)
William S Burroughs & Brion Gysin: The Third
    Mind (Viking Penguin, New York, 1978)

James Campbell: This is the Beat Generation
    (Secker & Warburg, London, 1999)
Samuel Taylor Coleridge: Christabel: Kubla Khan,
    a vision; The Pains of Sleep (John Murray,
    London, 1816)
Gregory Corso: Gasoline (City Lights, san
    Francisco, 1958)
Gregory Corso: The Happy Birthday of Death
    (New Directions, New York, 1960)
Gregory Corso: Long Live Man (New Directions,
    New York, 1962)
Gregory Corso: Selected Poems (Eyre &
    Spottiswoode, London, 1962)
Gregory Corso: An Accidental Autobiography
    - The Selected Letters of Gregory Corso
    (New Directions, New York, 2003)
John Yerbury Dent: Anxiety and Its Treatment -
    with Special Reference to Alcoholism (John
    Murray, London, 1941)
Lawrence Ferlinghetti: A Coney Island of the
    Mind (New Directions, New York, 1958)
Lawrence Ferlinghetti: San Francisco Poems (City
    Lights Foundation, San Francisco, 2001)
Jonathan Fryer: Soho in The Fifties & Sixties
    (National Portrait Gallery, London, 1998)
John Galsworthy: The Forsythe Saga (Charles
    Scribner's Sons, New York, 1922)
Allen Ginsberg: Howl (City Lights, San Francisco,
    1956)

Allen Ginsberg: Planet News (City Lights, San Francisco, 1968)

Allen Ginsberg: Collected Poems 1947-1980 (Harper & Row, New York, 1984)

Francis Bret Harte: The Luck of Roaring Camp, and Other Sketches (Fields, Osgood & Co, Boston, 1870)

Jack Kerouac: The Town and the City (Harcourt Brace & Co, New York, 1950)

Jack Kerouac: Lonesome Traveler (McGraw-Hill, New York, 1960)

Jack Kerouac: Desolation Angels (Coward-McCann, New York, 1965)

Jack Kerouac: Vanity of Dulouz (Coward-McCann, New York, 1968)

Jack Kerouac: Scattered Poems (City Lights, San Francisco, 1971)

Jack Kerouac: Selected Letters 1957-1969 (Viking Penguin, New York, 1999)

Herman Melville: Moby Dick; or, The Whale (Richard Bentley/Harper Brothers, New York, 1851)

Barry Miles: The Beat Hotel (Grove Press, New York, 2000)

Barry Miles: In the Sixties (Jonathan Cape, London, 2002)

Barry Miles: Beat Collection (Virgin Books, London, 2005)

Ted Morgan: Literary Outlaw - The Life and
    Times of William S. Burroughs (The Bodley
    Head, London, 1991)

Arthur Rimbaud & Wyatt Mason (Editor):
    Rimbaud Complete (Scribner, New York,
    2003)

Graham Robb: Rimbaud - A Biography (W W
    Norton & Co, New York, 2000)

Jack Sargeant: Naked Lens - An Illustrated
    History of Beat Cinema (Creation Books,
    London, 1997)

Percy Bysshe Shelley: The Poetical Works
    (Edward Moxon, London, 1839)

Bram Stoker: Dracula (Archibald Constable,
    London, 1867)

Roger Tagholm: Walking Literary London (New
    Holland Publishers, London, 2001)

Dylan Thomas: In Country Sleep and Other
    Poems (New Directions, New York, 1952)

Mark Twain: Adventures of Huckleberry Finn
    (Charles L Webster & Co, New York, 1885)

Joy Walsh (Editor): Moody Street Irregulars: A
    Jack Kerouac Newsletter (Clarence Center,
    New York 1978-1994)

Peter Whitehead: Wholly Communion - The Film
    (Lorrimer Films, London, 1965)

Thomas Wolfe: Look Homeward Angel (Charles
    Scribner's Sons, New York, 1929)

Websites

Appleseed Recordings - www.appleseedrec.com
Beat Books - www.beatbooks.com
The Beat Museum - www.thebeatmuseum.org
Beatles in London - www.beatlesinlondon.com
The British Museum -
        www.thebritishmuseum.ac.uk
Brompton Cemetery - www.royalparks.gov.uk/
parks/brompton_cemetery
Bunhill Fields - cityoflondon.gov.uk/Corporation/
living_environment/open_spaces/bunhill.htm
City Lights - www.citylights.com
Dharma Beat - www.wordsareimportant.com
Find A Grave - www.findagrave.com
Fool on a Hill - www.foolonahill.com
Allen Ginsberg - www.allenginsberg.org
Hoppy's Media Archives - www.hoppy.be
Institute of Contemporary Arts (ICA) -
        www.ica.org
Dr Johnson's House - www.drjh.dircon.co.uk
Jack Kerouac - www.jackerouac.com
The Jack Kerouac School of Disembodied
Poetics -
        naropa.edu/writingandpoetics/index.html
Literary Kicks - www.litkicks.com
London Blue Plaques -
        www.english-heritage.org.uk
New Directions Publishing Corp -
        www.ndpublishing.com

The Penguin Group - www.penguin.com
The Random House Group -
    www.randomhouse.com
Reality Studio - www.realitystudio.org
Regent's Park - www.royalparks.gov.uk/parks/
regents_park
Arthur Rimbaud - www.mag4net/Rimbaud
RookNet - www.rooknet.com
Royal Albert Hall - www.royalalberthall.com
Salon - www.salon.com
Percy Bysshe Shelley -
www.wam.umd.edu/~djb/shelley/home.html
Tate Galleries - www.tate.org.uk

Sources

Thanks are due to the following copyright holders for their permission to reprint:

Excerpts from *In The Sixties* by Barry Miles, published by Jonathan Cape. Reprinted by permission of The Anthony Harwood Agency.

Excerpts from *Literary Outlaw – The Life and Times of William S Burroughs* by Ted Morgan, published by The Bodley Head. Reprinted by permission of The Random House Group Ltd.

Excerpts from *With William Burroughs: A Report From The Bunker* by Victor Bockris, published by Vermilion. Reprinted by permission of The Random House Group Ltd.

Excerpts from *Vanity of Duluoz, Lonesome Traveler, Desolation Angels, Selected Letters 1957-1969 and Origins of the Beat Generation* by Jack Kerouac. Reprinted by permission of SII/ sterling Lord Literistic Inc, Copyright by Jack Kerouac.

Excerpts from *The Letters of William S Burroughs 1945-1959* by William S Burroughs, edited by Oliver Harris, copyright © 2003 by William S Burroughs. Used by permission of Viking Penguin, a division of Penguin Group (USA) Inc and by permission of Picador, a

Cast of Characters

Charles Addams	Walk 1
Captain Ahab	Walk 4
Prince Albert	Walk 1
Daevid Allen	Walk 4
Michelangelo Antonioni	Walk 5
Apollo	Walk 5
Holy Old Arab	Walk 5
David Archer	Walk 3
Angel in the Field	Walk 2
Jane Asher	Walk 2
Peter Asher	Walks 3 & 4
W H Auden	Walk 4
Henry Austen	Walk 5
Jane Austen	Walk 5
Antony Balch	Walks 1, 2, 3, 4 & 5
J G Ballard	Walks 1 & 4
George Barker	Walk 3
Sir John Barbirolli	Walks 1 & 2
J M Barrie	Walk 5
Clinking Bartenders	Walk 5
Gregory Bateson	Walk 2
Charles Baudelaire	Walks 2 & 5
Beatles	Walks 1, 2, 3 & 5
Samuel Beckett	Walk 5
Ambrose Bierce	Walk 1
Bird Man	Walk 4
William Blake	Walks 1, 2, 3 & 4
Bobbies (Policemen)	Walks 2 & 5
Victor Bockris	Walks 1, 2, 4 & 5
Bearded Bohemians	Walk 3
Marc Bolan	Walk 4
James Boswell	Walk 4
Sandro Botticelli	Walk 1
David Bowie	Walk 4

Paul Bowles	Walk 2
Arthur Boyars	Walk 1
Marion Boyars	Walk 1
Pete Brown	Walk 1
Tod Browning	Walk 1
Basil Bunting	Walk 3
John Bunyan	Walk 2
Anthony Burgess	Walk 4
William S Burroughs	Walks 1, 2, 3, 4 & 5
Bill Butler	Walk 3
Lord Byron	Walk 2
Cabaret Voltaire	Walk 5
John Calder	Walks 1 & 3
Neal Cassady	Walk 4
Giggling Old Tao Chinaman	Walk 5
Henry Cohen	Walk 5
Samuel Taylor Coleridge	Walk 1
Cyril Connolly	Walk 5
Control	Walk 1
Joseph Conrad	Walk 5
Peter Cook	Walk 5
Michael Cooper	Walk 5
Gregory Corso	Walks 1, 2, 3, 4 & 5
Snarling Counterman	Walk 3
Aleister Crowley	Walks 4 & 5
George Nathanial Curzon	Walk 4
Dancing Girl	Walk 1
Peter Davies	Walk 5
David Dawson	Walk 5
Francisco De Miranda	Walk 3
Thomas De Quincey	Walk 3
Daniel Defoe	Walk 2
Dr Dent	Walks 1, 2 & 5
Andre Deutsch	Walk 3
Moby Dick	Walk 4
Charles Dickens	Walk 3
Donovan	Walks 3 & 4

Ernest Dowson	Walk 3
Count Dracula	Walk 5
Dr Dunbar	Walk 4
John Dunbar	Walk 4
Bob Dylan	Walks 1, 2, 4 & 5
The Egg Man	Walk 4
Lord Elgin	Walk 3
T S Eliot	Walk 1
Queen Elizabeth	Walks 2 & 4
Roger Ely	Walk 5
Eros	Walk 3
Harry Fainlight	Walk 1
Marianne Faithfull	Walk 2
Guy Fawkes	Walk 4
Julie Felix	Walks 3 & 5
Lawrence Ferlinghetti	Walks 1, 2, 3, 4 & 5
Fool on the Hill	Walk 2
George Fox	Walk 2
Benjamin Franklin	Walk 4
Clark Gable	Walk 5
John Galsworthy	Walk 4
Indira Gandhi	Walk 1
Gas Man	Walk 2
David Gascoyne	Walk 3
Jean Genet	Walk 5
Christopher Gibbs	Walk 5
Allen Ginsberg	Walks 1, 2, 3, 4 & 5
Louis Ginsberg	Walk 4
John Giorno	Walk 5
Gog & Magog	Walk 4
The Golem	Walk 5
Panna Grady	Walks 2 & 4
El Greco	Walk 4
Griffin	Walk 4
Arthur Grimble	Walk 1
Guardsman Type & Lady	Walk 5
Guru	Walk 2

Brion Gysin	Walks 1, 3, 4 & 5
Hall Manager	Walk 1
Patrick Hamilton	Walk 1
Oliver Hardy	Walk 5
Keith Haring	Walk 3
George Harrison	Walks 1 & 2
Patti Harrison	Walk 2
Francis Bret Harte	Walk 1
Hassan-i-Sabbah	Walks 1 & 4
Joan Haverty	Walk 2
Jimi Hendrix	Walk 2
Adrian Henri	Walk 1
Ian Hinchliffe	Walk 5
John Cam Hobhouse	Walk 2
Hodge	Walk 4
Michael Hollingshead	Walk 5
Anselm Hollo	Walks 1 & 5
John Clellon Holmes	Walk 5
John 'Hoppy' Hopkins	Walk 1
Jack Horner	Walk 3
Michael Horovitz	Walks 1 & 4
Horsa	Walk 4
White Horse	Walk 2
L Ron Hubbard	Walk 3
Hunchback	Walk 2
Bianca Jagger	Walk 4
Mick Jagger	Walks 1, 2 & 4
Ernst Jandl	Walk 1
Derek Jarman	Walk 3
Sir Cowasjee Jehangir	Walk 2
Dr Johnson	Walk 4
Krazy Kat	Walk 5
LeRoi Jones	Walk 4
Julian	Walk 4
Lebris de Keroack	Walk 3
Jack Kerouac	Walks 1, 2, 3, 4 & 5

R D Laing	Walks 1, 2 & 5
Philip Lamantia	Walks 1 & 2
George Lamming	Walk 1
Lillie Langtry	Walk 1
Philip Larkin	Walk 3
James Laughlin	Walks 1 & 5
Stan Laurel	Walk 5
Robert LaVigne	Walk 5
Cynthia Lennon	Walk 2
John Lennon	Walks 1, 2 & 4
Liberal MP	Walk 1
Lillian	Walk 3
Christopher Logue	Walk 1
Gina Lollabrigida	Walk 3
Sterling Lord	Walk 3
Old King Lud	Walk 4
Douglas Lyne	Walks 1, 4 & 5
Monica Lyne	Walk 1
Lady Macbeth	Walk 4
Maid	Walk 3
Gerard Malanga	Walk 3
Martha	Walk 2
Grouch Marx	Walk 3
Queen Mary	Walk 3
Sir Robery Mayer	Walk 2
Linda McCartney	Walk 4
Paul McCartney	Walks 1, 2, 4 & 5
Michael McClure	Walk 2
Hazel Guggenheim McKinley	Walk 5
Meacher, Higgins & Thomas	Walk 2
Herman Melville	Walk 4
Barry Miles	Walks 1, 2, 3 & 4
Sue Miles	Walks 2 & 3
John Everett Millais	Walk 5
Henry Miller	Walk 3
Adrian Mitchell	Walks 1 & 4

Dudley Moore	Walk 5
Tom Moore	Walk 2
Ted Morgan	Walks 1, 3 & 4
Wolfgang Amadeus Mozart	Walk 5
John Murray	Walk 2
Lord Nelson	Walk 4
Pablo Neruda	Walk 1
Bob Neuwirth	Walk 4
Twinkling Newspaperman	Walk 4
Jeff Nuttall	Walks 1 & 5
Charles Olson	Walks 2 & 4
Yoko Ono	Walks 2 & 4
Peter Orlovsky	Walks 1 & 3
George Orwell	Walk 3
Sonia Orwell	Walks 3 & 4
Peter Pan	Walks 1 & 5
Giant Panda, Lions, Humming Birds & Ladies	Walk 2
Kenneth Patchen	Walks 4 & 5
Psychiatric Patients	Walk 1
Brian Patten	Walk 1
Ivan Pavlov	Walk 4
Paxton & Whitfield	Walk 4
D A Pennebaker	Walks 1 & 4
Charming Street Performers	Walk 3
Saint-John Perse	Walk 2
Tom Pickard	Walk 4
J Kingson Pierce	Walk 1
Pigeons, Lions & Unicorns	Walk 4
Pink Floyd	Walk 2
Mike Plumbley	Walk 3
Edgar Allen Poe	Walk 5
Roman Polanski	Walk 5
Genesis P-Orridge	Walks 3, 4 & 5
Mikey Portman	Walks 2 & 5
Madame Prunier	Walk 4

Psychic TV	Walk 5
Kenneth Rexroth	Walk 2
Arthur Rimbaud	Walks 2, 3 & 5
The Rolling Stones	Walk 1
Barbara Rubin	Walk 1
Quiet Sage	Walk 5
Anthony Salvin	Walk 2
Edie Sedgwick	Walk 3
George Seferis	Walk 5
Simon Seligman	Walk 4
William Shakespeare	Walks 1 & 5
Percy Bysshe Shelley	Walk 3
Shiva	Walk 1
Shopkeepers, Waiters, Hotel Clerks & Doormen	Walk 4
Edith Sitwell	Walks 2 & 4
Stevie Smith	Walk 3
John Snow	Walk 3
Gary Snyder	Walk 2
Soft Machine	Walk 2
Drinking Soldier	Walk 3
Four Quartets Soldier	Walks 1 & 3
Ian Sommerville	Walks 1, 2, 3, 4 & 5
Stephen Spender	Walk 4
Ringo Starr	Walk 2
Jacques Stern	Walk 2
Bram Stoker	Walk 5
The Subliminal Kid	Walk 1
Swan & Edgar	Walk 3
Swans, Ducks & Gulls	Walk 1
Taffy	Walk 4
Sharon Tate	Walk 5
Teddy Boys	Walk 3
Thespis, Ceres & Graces	Walk 3
Caitlin Thomas	Walks 3 & 5
Dylan Thomas	Walks 2, 3 & 5

Mrs Thrale	Walk 4
Ruthven Todd	Walk 2
Alexander Trocchi	Walks 1, 3 & 5
Anthony Trollope	Walk 2
Peter Ilyich Tchaikovsky	Walk 1
J M W Turner	Walk 5
Mark Twain	Walk 5
Giuseppe Ungaretti	Walk 4
Paul Verlaine	Walks 2 & 3
Simon Vinkenoog	Walk 1
Violent Hash Smoker	Walk 3
Sad Violinists	Walk 3
Andrei Voznesensky	Walk 1 & 3
Waiters in Tuxedos	Walk 5
Anne Waldman	Walk 4
Andy Warhol	Walks 3 & 4
Alan Watson	Walk 4
George Frederick Watts	Walk 1
Duke of Wellington	Walk 2
H G Wells	Walks 2 & 5
Werewolf of London	Walk 5
John Wesley	Walk 2
Philip Whalen	Walks 2 & 3
Anna McNeill Whistler	Walk 5
James McNeill Whistler	Walk 5
Ed White	Walk 4
Peter Whitehead	Walks 1 & 3
Oscar Wilde	Walk 5
Ralph Vaughan Williams	Walk 2
Thomas Wolfe	Walk 5
Young Woman at the Bar	Walk 5
Seymour Wyse	Walks 1, 2 & 5
Yevgeny Yevtushenko	Walk 3
Turtleneck Youths	Walk 3
Count Zinzendorf	Walk 5

Printed in the United Kingdom
by Lightning Source UK Ltd.
109156UKS00001BA/4-18